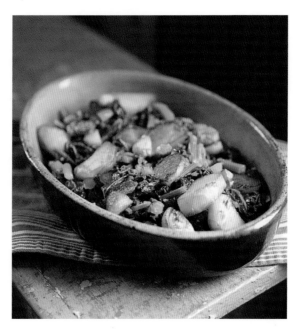

ITALIAN
COMFORT FOOD

ITALIAN
COMFORT FOOD

125 RECIPES TO SATISFY YOUR SOUL

JULIA DELLA CROCE

PHOTOGRAPHS BY CHRISTOPHER HIRSHEIMER

KYLE CATHIE LTD

For my father, born Giovanni Giuseppe della Croce,
April 13, 1908, Toritto, Puglia, Italy; died John Dellacroce,
February 1, 2008, Suffern, New York, U.S.A.

First published in 2010 by Kyle Cathie Limited,
23 Howland Street, London W1T 4AY
general.enquiries@kyle-cathie.com
www.kylecathie.com

978-1-85626-936-0

Text © 2010 Julia della Groce
Food photography © 2010 Christopher Hirsheimer
Location photography © 2010 Paolo Destefanis
Book design © 2010 Kyle Cathie Limited

Project editor Anja Schmidt
Designer Sara Schneider
Photographer Christopher Hirsheimer
Styling Melissa Hamilton
Copyeditor Janet McDonald
Production Lisa Pinnell and Gemma John

A CIP catalogue record for this title is available
from the British Library.

Colour reproduction by Sang Choy
Printed and bound in China by C & C Offset Printing Co.

Contents

INTRODUCTION

'In Italy, food is considered to be good only
in homes where there is an old lady wearing
slippers in the kitchen.'

— *Francesco Antonucci, chef and restaurateur, Remi, 2005*

In the summer of 1967, I made my first trip to Italy to meet family I'd never known. I immediately felt that I'd come home. The sea of Sardinia, the light, the colours, all cast a spell over me and the people captured my heart. And then there was the food! Newly discovered relatives overwhelmed my senses with local dishes: Zia Anna preparing a rabbit and olive stew; Zia Nella a capon with bread, sausage and saffron stuffing; cousin Ida a suckling pig roasted on a bed of myrtle leaves. On Sundays, we piled into boats on the Cagliari Bay and plucked sea urchins from their pink coral beds, anointing our catch with juice from the fat lemons we'd picked along the coastal road. The food was better than anything I'd eaten before.

Since then, whether living abroad or in America, I have been drawn to the delights and comforts of Italian food. I have been nourished by it and, in turn, have nourished others with it. There is nothing about it that I do not love. Even the rituals of preparation and the rhythms of the harvest season bring comfort and anticipation, like the swish of the mezzaluna blade mincing the *battuto* on a wooden cutting board for Sunday ragù, or the robust cadence of the market as men set up their produce stalls early in the morning. But what I would not have imagined half a century ago has become a reality: home cooking is disappearing now that so many women, the customary standard bearers of culinary traditions, are in the workforce.

Historically, Italian cooking has been a feminine art – an expression of creativity and imagination even when resources were scarce. With the food close at hand – in the garden or foraged from the countryside, from the hunter's catch or the fisherman's haul – women created a cuisine that has lasted millennia and captured more souls than the Roman Empire – without bloodshed.

Who will be the guardians of cooking traditions now? Much *alta cucina* is so astonishing in its technical achievement and aesthetic sophistication that its flavour seems almost secondary. Today, most culinary school graduates want to invent contemporary gastronomy, not reproduce the cooking of their grandmothers.

The rapid technological changes of modern life make it even more important for us to remember the exquisite sense of well-being, the warmth and excitement we once derived from eating food slowly and lovingly cooked at home. This book is an homage to that kind of food; to the kitchens of the Italian people, my own family of devoted cooks included, who have developed and preserved Italian cooking through the centuries and – during waves of immigration – across oceans to new worlds. Those fortunate enough to have eaten in an Italian home where an 'old lady wearing slippers' still possesses the knowledge of these food traditions will understand what others have missed. In America, we call it 'comfort food'. The Italians call it *cucina casalinga*, 'home cuisine', and it is a highly evolved art form. It is the Italian food I love best, and you will find it in these pages.

AUTHOR'S NOTE TO THIS VOLUME:

The question inevitably arises about what dishes are traditional and what dishes are not. Because cuisine is a living craft based on products of the earth, it is always changing. The availability of foods, modern agricultural practices, dietary trends, foreign and cultural influences, and our current environmental responsibilities are just a few of the evolutionary factors in play. But whether recipes are part of a family's heritage or are newly created, there remains an essential difference between home cooking – comfort food – and professional cooking. *Cucina casalinga* is casual and relaxed, designed to sustain the body and uplift the spirit. Readers will find that this collection of recipes reflects the rustic, simple elegance of the best in Italian comfort food.

1

WELCOMING DISHES:
APPETISERS, SAVOURIES AND SNACKS

Italians are nurturing and hospitable, especially at the table. Of welcoming dishes there is no end, and almost no end to their names, too. Called *spuntini* (from the verb meaning 'spring up', suggesting spontaneity) or *intermezzi* ('interludes'), and most often *antipasti* (literally, 'before the meal'), they are appetisers at meals or snacks in between. Italians love to *pizzicare* (to 'pick at') many dishes on the table, sampling instead of overindulging. Several *antipasti* can combine as a light meal on their own. If pasta is served at lunch, dinner is often light, served with side dishes such as the ones I've included in this chapter. *Antipasti* are informal pleasures – creative but casual in their many forms: *salumi (prosciutto, speck, mortadella, coppa, salami* and other cold cuts), vegetable compotes, breads and pies, *bruschette* and *crostini,* salads (see Chapter 3), and fritters beyond counting. I confess that I love them all, and some of my favourites are offered here.

CREAMY AUBERGINE SPREAD
ON BRUSCHETTA

Serves 4

The Italians have so many delicious ways of cooking aubergines, but this, perhaps one of the simplest, is a favourite of my daughter, a vegetarian. The clear flavours of fresh aubergine and good olive oil pop because no herbs or spices distract except for a pinch of oregano. The trick to transforming aubergine from bitter to sweet without salting it is to remove excess seeds after roasting or barbecuing (if charred on a wood-fired barbecue, the pulp will take on a pleasant smoky flavour).

2 MEDIUM ITALIAN AUBERGINES

4 GARLIC CLOVES, UNPEELED

2 TEASPOONS WHITE WINE VINEGAR

6 TABLESPOONS EXTRA-VIRGIN OLIVE OIL

½ TEASPOON SEA SALT

FRESHLY GROUND BLACK PEPPER

FRESHLY SLICED AND TOASTED ARTISAN BREAD, TO SERVE

¼ TEASPOON DRIED OREGANO, CRUSHED

1. Preheat the oven to 200°C/400°F/gas mark 6.

2. Place the whole aubergines and garlic cloves on a baking tray and slide the tray onto the middle rack of the oven. Roast the garlic until soft, about 15 minutes; remove from the oven and set aside. Roast the aubergines until completely soft and collapsed and the skin is blackened, about 40 minutes. Remove from the oven and allow to cool. Use a spoon to scoop and discard excess seeds from the aubergines. Put the pulp in a sieve and leave it to drain to release excess moisture, from 1 hour to overnight, chilled.

3. Peel and mash the garlic and place it and the aubergine pulp in the bowl of an electric mixer. Alternatively, place it in a mixing bowl and use a hand whisk. Add the vinegar. Use the whisk attachment, or whisking by hand, whisk the mixture while pouring in the olive oil little by little, as though you were making mayonnaise, until the aubergine mixture is creamy and light. Season with salt and pepper.

4. Spread the aubergine cream onto the warm toasted bread slices. Sprinkle with oregano and serve.

AHEAD-OF-TIME NOTE: This spread can be made well ahead of time and stored in a covered container, chilled, for up to 5 days.

BATTER-FRIED
SAGE LEAVES AND COURGETTE FLOWERS

Serves 4

My family looks forward to summer every year when we can make these beautiful little treats from the courgette flowers and sage out of our garden (once fried, sage loses its pungency but not its flavour). They are so easy to make and nearly foolproof if you use the right ingredients. You can serve them for snacks, as appetisers, or as a side dish with dinner; guests invariably love them. The combination of courgette flowers and sage is a happy union, but you can make either one separately. When courgette flowers aren't available, it is easy enough to find fresh sage year-round in the herb section of the supermarket.

PURE (NOT EXTRA VIRGIN) OLIVE, GRAPESEED OR OTHER VEGETABLE OIL WITH A HIGH SMOKING POINT, FOR FRYING

60G UNBLEACHED PLAIN FLOUR

12 TABLESPOONS SPARKLING MINERAL WATER

12 COURGETTE FLOWERS WITH ABOUT 5CM OF STEM LEFT INTACT

16 LARGE SAGE LEAVES WITH ABOUT 2.5CM OF STEM LEFT INTACT

SEA SALT

1. Fill a deep frying pan with enough oil to reach about 2.5cm up the sides. Warm over medium heat until the oil is hot enough to make a sage leaf sizzle when dropped in.

2. In the meantime, put the flour into a mixing bowl large enough to accommodate a flower. Pour in the sparkling water and mix with a whisk until the mixture is blended and smooth. It should have the consistency of beaten egg and easily coat a spoon. If the mixture is too thick, thin with a little more of the water.

3. Begin with the courgette flowers. Wash the flowers rapidly under cold running water and dry them gently on kitchen paper; check inside the flowers for insects; remove the stamens. Dip each of the flowers into the batter just before you are ready to cook them, using the stem as a handle for slipping them into the pan. Put only as many flowers or leaves into the oil as can fit without crowding. Fry until golden, about 3 minutes altogether, turning them over midway during cooking. Use a skimmer to retrieve them when they are done. Transfer to kitchen paper, taking care not to spread the flowers to avoid crushing them. Sprinkle them with salt immediately to ensure it will stick and keep them crisp. Follow the same procedure for frying and salting the sage leaves, only frying them about 1 minute. Serve at once.

STUFFED
COURGETTE FLOWERS
Serves 4

I grow plentiful courgettes in my garden to ensure that there will be enough flowers to satisfy my craving for them. This is one of my favourite ways of preparing them, learned as a girl by watching my aunt make them after our forays to the open-air markets near her apartment in Rome. Select flowers that are about 7.5cm from the base of the flower to their tips.

PURE OLIVE OIL, FOR FRYING

60G UNBLEACHED PLAIN FLOUR

12 TABLESPOONS SPARKLING MINERAL WATER

16 LARGE COURGETTE FLOWERS WITH ABOUT 5CM OF STEM LEFT INTACT

110G FRESH MOZZARELLA, GENUINE CACIOCAVALLO OR GENUINE ASIAGO FRESCO, CUT INTO 16 DICE

SEA SALT

1. Fill a deep frying pan with enough oil to reach about 4cm up the sides. Warm the oil over medium heat until it is sizzling hot.

2. Meanwhile, put the flour into a mixing bowl large enough for a flower to fit. Pour in the sparkling water and mix with a whisk until the mixture is blended and smooth. It should have the consistency of beaten egg and easily coat a spoon. If the mixture is too thick, thin with a little more of the water.

3. Wash the flowers rapidly under cold running water and dry them gently on kitchen paper; check inside the flowers for insects; remove the stamens. Slip a piece of cheese into each, then fold the flower closed, pressing gently to make the petals adhere to each other.

4. Just before you are ready to cook them, dip each of the flowers into the batter, using the stem as a handle for slipping them into the pan. Put only as many flowers into the oil as can fit without crowding. Fry until golden, about 5 minutes in all, turning them over midway during cooking. Use a skimmer to retrieve them when they are done. Transfer to kitchen paper, taking care to avoid crushing them. Sprinkle with salt immediately to ensure it will stick and keep the flowers crisp. Serve at once.

OLIVE
PESTO
Serves 4

Few things are more evocative of childhood in an Italian home than olives, particularly luscious black olives from the southern regions. In our home, they studded pumpkin stew, pasta sauces, chicken casseroles, thick *baccalà* chowder and countless other dishes. One can rely on olives to enliven just about anything, but they can also stand alone, such as in the pesto I devised for a tasty topping for anything from crackers or crusty bread to pasta or grilled fish. If you keep brine-cured pitted olives in your pantry, it takes only minutes to make. For a more elaborate version, you can add three anchovies, the zest of one lemon, a small finely chopped red onion, and a couple of tablespoons of finely chopped fresh parsley.

360G PITTED BRINE-CURED BLACK OLIVES SUCH AS GAETA, KALAMATA, OR NIÇOISE

2 TEASPOONS FINELY CHOPPED FRESH MARJORAM OR 1 TEASPOON DRIED MARJORAM

1 LARGE GARLIC CLOVE, FINELY GRATED

60ML EXTRA-VIRGIN OLIVE OIL, PLUS ADDITIONAL, IF NEEDED

THINLY SLICED, FRESHLY TOASTED PLAIN ARTISAN BREAD OR PLAIN SALTED CRACKERS, TO SERVE

1. In the bowl of a food processor, combine the olives, marjoram, garlic and olive oil. Pulse to grind 3 to 4 seconds. The resulting mixture should have some texture. Avoid over-pulsing, which will make the mixture too pasty and smooth. Transfer to a small but ample serving bowl and stir in more extra-virgin olive oil, if needed.

2. Spread the pesto onto the warm toasted bread slices and serve.

AHEAD-OF-TIME NOTE: This spread can be made well ahead of time and stored in a fridge for up to 3 weeks.

CLASSIC
SICILIAN CAPONATA
Serves 4

This stellar sweet-and-sour aubergine compote is a staple on the Sicilian table, as it was on ours, despite my mother's Sardinian origin. Caponata is typically served as an appetiser in Sicily, but we children ate it happily as an after-school snack or a pick-me-up at any time of day. Serve it on lettuce leaves or freshly toasted slices of bread.

450G ITALIAN AUBERGINES

SEA SALT

PURE OLIVE OIL, FOR DEEP-FRYING

3 TABLESPOONS EXTRA-VIRGIN OLIVE OIL

1 LARGE ONION, CHOPPED

4 LARGE GARLIC CLOVES, SMASHED

5 CELERY STICKS, STRINGS REMOVED, CUT INTO 2.5-CM DICE

2 TABLESPOONS ITALIAN CAPERS PACKED IN SALT, RINSED THOROUGHLY

1½ TABLESPOONS TART GREEN SICILIAN OLIVES, PITTED AND QUARTERED

300ML CRUSHED TOMATOES OR PASSATA

1 TABLESPOON RED WINE VINEGAR, OR MORE TO TASTE

1 TABLESPOON SUGAR

FRESHLY GROUND BLACK PEPPER TO TASTE

3 TABLESPOONS FINELY CHOPPED FRESH BASIL

LETTUCE LEAVES OR TOASTED BREAD SLICES, TO SERVE

1. Wash the aubergines and remove the stem and navel. Leave the skin on. Cut into 2.5-cm cubes and transfer to a colander. Sprinkle lightly with salt and place a dish with a weight on top. Place the colander in a clean sink or on a plate where it can drain unhampered for at least 1 hour to give the seeds time to release their bitter liquid. Pat the aubergine well with kitchen paper to blot moisture and salt.

2. Pour enough olive oil to reach 2.5cm up the sides of a frying pan. When it is sizzling hot, add the aubergine and fry until coloured and soft, about 5 minutes. Drain on kitchen paper and sprinkle immediately with sea salt; set aside.

3. In a frying pan, warm the 3 tablespoons olive oil. Add the onion and garlic and sauté over medium heat until wilted, about 5 minutes. Add the celery and sauté until coloured but still crisp, about 5 minutes. Add the aubergine, capers and olives and toss. Stir in the tomatoes or passata, vinegar, sugar, pepper and basil. Cook over low heat for 10 minutes. Cover and chill overnight to develop the flavours.

4. Check for seasoning before serving. Caponata is best eaten at room temperature. Serve on lettuce leaves or toasted bread.

AHEAD-OF-TIME NOTE: Caponata will keep for 1 week, chilled.

BAKED CLAMS
WITH BACON
Serves 4

Few dishes are more emblematic of the Italian-American family-style restaurant than baked clams. Italian clams are about the size of a man's thumbnail, so it is not surprising that this dish is never presented in Italy. Only the larger Eastern Littleneck clams are suitable for stuffing. The clams should not be larger than 3cm in diameter or they will be too tough.

24 LIVE LITTLENECK CLAMS

100G SEA SALT OR KOSHER SALT

150G CORNMEAL

FOR THE TOPPING

2 TABLESPOONS EXTRA-VIRGIN OLIVE OIL

1 LARGE GARLIC CLOVE, FINELY CHOPPED OR PASSED THROUGH A GARLIC PRESS

2 TABLESPOONS FINE DRIED BREAD CRUMBS

2 TABLESPOONS CHOPPED FRESH ROASTED OR BOTTLED ROASTED SWEET RED PEPPER

2 TEASPOONS CHOPPED FRESH FLAT-LEAF PARSLEY

110G FINELY CHOPPED PANCETTA OR BACON

DRY WHITE WINE, FOR SPRINKLING

2 LEMONS, CUT INTO WEDGES

1. Soak the clams for 3 to 4 hours in 4 litres of water mixed with the sea salt and cornmeal. (Use sea salt or kosher salt, as the iodine in regular salt will kill them.) One hour before cooking, scrub and rinse the clams well with a stiff vegetable brush under cold running water until they are free of sand. Tap any open clams. If they close, keep them; if not, discard at once. Place the clams in a bowl of hot water for 10 minutes to facilitate opening. Meanwhile, preheat the grill.

2. In a mixing bowl combine all the ingredients for the topping and mix well. Working over a bowl to catch any clam juice, insert a clam knife or a small, sturdy paring knife between a clam's shells and, with a horizontal movement, thrust the blade toward the muscle on the base of the shell to open it. Detach the flesh from the shell cavity to make it easier to lift out when eating. Leave the whole clam meat in one of its shells and discard the other shell. Repeat with the other clams.

3. Spoon an equal amount of the topping over each clam. Drizzle a little of the clam juice from the bowl over the topping, then sprinkle lightly with a little wine to keep the clams moist. Place the clams in a heatproof baking dish 20cm from the grill. Grill for 6 minutes, watching carefully so the topping does not burn. If it browns too quickly, move the rack further from the grill and add a little more clam juice or wine before returning to the grill. Serve hot with lemon wedges.

CRISPY LITTLE
CALZONE
Makes 8 calzone

Yeast dough is delicious fried, and these homey calzone (literally, 'big socks') shouldn't be overlooked in the repertoire of appetisers and snack food for children and adults alike (kids love them as much as they love pizza). Fillings can be as simple as anchovy fillets or slices of good *salame,* or a combination of ham or *salame* and mozzarella, which melt into a pleasing ooziness when the calzone are hot. You can bake them, if you prefer; see the note below.

1 RECIPE RAPHAEL ZOERI'S MILK DOUGH
FOR YEAST BREAD (PAGE 216)

SALAME, PROSCIUTTO, OR A GOOD
ITALIAN MELTING CHEESE SUCH AS
MOZZARELLA, CACIOCAVALLO, FONTINA
OR STRACCHINO

OLIVE OIL OR VEGETABLE OIL, FOR FRYING

SEA SALT

1. Make the dough as directed; divide into pieces the size of a small peach. Stretch each piece out into a thin, 15-cm round.

2. Place a piece of salame, prosciutto or cheese, or a combination of both, in the centre and fold the disc in half. Moisten the edges with a little water and seal shut. Crimp the edges well to prevent the filling from leaking out.

3. Pour enough oil into a frying pan to reach about 2.5cm up the sides. When it is hot enough to make the dough sizzle, slip the calzone into the pan and fry until golden brown on both sides (about 5 minutes in total). Don't skimp on the oil, because at least 2.5cm is needed for the calzone to fry properly on both sides. Drain on kitchen paper. Sprinkle with sea salt while still very hot. Serve at once.

NOTE: To bake, preheat the oven to 200°C/400°F/gas mark 6. Place the calzone on an oiled baking sheet and cook until golden, about 20 minutes.

RAPHAEL BOERI'S
PISSALADELLA
Makes 1

Here is a pizza-like flatbread much like one my paternal grandmother used to make as a treat for her eleven children. Even when times were lean, flour, yeast and onions were not hard to come by. Her rustic version had origins in Puglia, where she was born, but there are many versions throughout Italy, such as this one, which I learned from Italian pastry chef Raphael Boeri. His yeast dough is enriched with milk and egg, which makes the pastry light and flaky. The onions cook very slowly in olive oil and water without caramelising, which creates a very sweet, creamy and nourishing topping. Please *don't* skimp on the anchovy paste here – it virtually melts into the olive oil and becomes indistinguishable on the topping except for the remarkable flavour it imparts. For a zestier version, scatter brine-cured black olives or whole anchovy fillets over the topping after baking.

1 RECIPE RAPHAEL BOERI'S MILK DOUGH FOR YEAST BREAD (PAGE 216)

EXTRA-VIRGIN OLIVE OIL, FOR OILING

FOR THE TOPPING

8 ONIONS, HALVED AND SLICED PAPER-THIN

120ML EXTRA-VIRGIN OLIVE OIL, LESS 2 TABLESPOONS RESERVED

120ML WATER

2 TABLESPOONS ANCHOVY PASTE

1 TEASPOON FINELY CHOPPED FRESH OREGANO, OR ½ TEASPOON DRIED CRUMBLED OREGANO

1 TEASPOON SEA SALT

FRESHLY GROUND BLACK PEPPER

2 LARGE VINE-RIPE TOMATOES, CUT INTO THIN SLICES

90G PITTED AND SLICED KALAMATA OR GAETA OLIVES, OR 12 ANCHOVY FILLETS (OPTIONAL)

1. Make the dough as directed on page 216. While it is rising, lightly oil a 30.5 x 43-cm baking tray, or its equivalent; set aside.

2. Make the topping: combine the onions, olive oil and water in an ample pan. Cover and cook over low heat until soft and creamy, 45 minutes, stirring frequently to prevent the onions from sticking to the bottom of the pan. Turn off the heat. Blend the 2 reserved tablespoons of olive oil with the anchovy paste and stir it into the onions, mixing thoroughly; season with the oregano, salt and plenty of pepper.

3. Preheat the oven to 200°C/400°F/gas mark 6. On a lightly floured work surface, use a rolling pin to roll out the dough as thin as you can, forming it into a rectangular shape that will fit the dimensions of the baking tray; it should be no more than 5mm thick. Roll the dough up onto the rolling pin, lift it into place on the baking sheet, and unroll it into the tray. Go all around the tray, easing the

dough in. Press out air pockets with your fingertips and use a fork to prick holes all over the surface. Using a sharp knife or kitchen scissors, trim off excess dough around the rim *after* leaving a 2.5-cm overhang all around. Use dough scraps for making a bun and bake it. (Note that while the *pissaladella* does not need to rise for a second time, the bun will need a second rise until double in size before baking.) Line the dough with a layer of sliced tomatoes.

4. Turn the still-hot onion topping out onto the tomatoes and use a rubber spatula to spread it evenly; allow it to rest for 5 minutes, then slide the *pissaladella* onto the middle rack of the oven. Bake until the edges are golden, 20 to 25 minutes. Take it out of the oven and arrange the olives or anchovy fillets on top, if using. Allow the bread to settle for 15 minutes. Use a pastry wheel or sharp knife to cut it into tidy squares. Eat hot or warm.

NONNA GIULIA'S
LAMB AND ARTICHOKE EMPANADAS
Makes about 18

If you like meat pies, as I do, you'll love these empanadas, an heirloom recipe of my maternal grandmother and namesake, Giulia Esu. While they may sound more Spanish than Italian, empanadas are a legacy of Alghero, the ancient Spanish-built port on the island of Sardinia. The filling is the original, but the pastry recipe (page 219), developed by my friend, food writer and pastry expert Susan Purdy, has evolved from a lard-based *millefoglie* into a richly flavoured pie-type pastry. Pork or beef can be substituted for lamb with excellent results.

1 RECIPE NEW WORLD FLAKY PASTRY DOUGH (PAGE 219)

600G LEAN BONELESS LAMB

2 TABLESPOONS EXTRA-VIRGIN OLIVE OIL

1 MEDIUM ONION, CHOPPED

2 LARGE GARLIC CLOVES, FINELY CHOPPED

175G ROUGHLY CHOPPED COOKED FRESH OR FROZEN ARTICHOKE HEARTS

110G STALE BREAD

125ML STOCK OR MILK, FOR SOAKING BREAD

4 TABLESPOONS CHOPPED FRESH FLAT-LEAF PARSLEY

35G FRESHLY GRATED PECORINO, PARMIGIANO-REGGIANO OR GRANA PADANO CHEESE

2 LARGE EGG YOLKS (RESERVE EGG WHITES)

¾ TEASPOON SALT

¼ TEASPOON FRESHLY GROUND BLACK OR WHITE PEPPER

1 TABLESPOON CHOPPED FRESH ROSEMARY, OR 1½ TEASPOONS DRIED ROSEMARY

FOR THE EGG WASH

1 WHOLE EGG BEATEN WITH 1 TEASPOON WATER

1. Make the pastry and chill.

2. To make the filling, dice the lamb and mince it in the bowl of a food-processor fitted with a metal blade.

3. In a frying pan, warm the oil. Add the onion, garlic and artichokes and sauté over medium heat until the onion is wilted, 3 to 4 minutes. Add the meat and sauté gently until lightly browned on the surface and bright pink inside, about 2 minutes. Transfer the mixture to a medium bowl.

4. Trim the crusts off the bread. Place it in a bowl and pour in enough stock or milk to cover. Soak until softened. Squeeze the bread dry and crumble it; discard the stock or milk.

5. Add the crumbled bread, parsley, grated cheese, egg yolks, salt, pepper and rosemary to the meat mixture. Mix well.

6. Preheat the oven to 190°C/375°F/gas mark 5. Line 2 baking trays with greaseproof paper. On a floured work surface, roll out the dough until just less than 5mm thick. Using a 7.5-cm pastry cutter, stamp out as many rounds as possible from the dough. Transfer to the prepared baking trays. Gather the scraps together; roll out again and stamp out additional discs. Brush the rounds with the reserved egg whites.

7. Place a generous tablespoon of the filling in the centre of each dough disc. Fold the dough over the filling to create a half-moon shaped empanada, lining up the edges. Use a fork to firmly crimp the edges. Use extra dough to make decorations. Brush the surface with the egg wash. Bake until golden, about 30 minutes. Serve warm.

PANINI
WITH FRESH MOZZARELLA, TOMATO AND PESTO

Makes 4

A *panino* (*panini,* plural) is a sandwich. I originally created this sensational one for school-children. Despite their unfamiliarity with some of the ingredients (the pesto and the artisan bread), it became one of their favourite meals. For the sandwich shell, I use Roman pizza-by-the-yard, also called 'pizza bianca', that is typical of Roman bakeries. Outside of the borders of Italy and New York City, where baker Jim Lahey, formerly of Sullivan Street Bakery fame, popularised this sensational bread, it is not yet well known. If you cannot find this superb thin, light and flaky artisanal bread, substitute a good artisanal focaccia that can be sliced open horizontally to produce thin sandwich bread with a nice top and bottom crust. Alternatively, use *ciabatta*.

FLAT ARTISAN BREAD SUCH AS *PIZZA BIANCA*, FOCACCIA OR *CIABATTA* FOR 4 PEOPLE

2 TABLESPOONS BASIL PESTO (PAGE 44)

1 LARGE FRESH, VINE-RIPENED TOMATO, CORED AND THINLY SLICED

SEA SALT, TO TASTE

225G FRESHLY MADE MOZZARELLA, SLICED INTO 4 SLICES OF THE SAME SIZE

1. If using a flatbread, cut into 4 equal serving-size rectangles or squares. Then cut the bread in half horizontally to obtain a bottom and top. If using *ciabatta* or other artisan bread, slice a standard portion size from the loaf for each person and slice it open like a book.

2. To assemble the sandwich, first smear a little pesto on the cut sides of both top and bottom bread slices. Lay a tomato slice over it and sprinkle with salt. Over that, lay the mozzarella slice. Put the lid on the sandwich and cut in half.

AUBERGINE
FRITTERS

Serves 4

A classic in the Italian fritter repertoire, these aubergine morsels are always a big hit whenever I serve them. They ooze comfort on a cold day.

PURE OLIVE OIL, FOR GREASING TRAY AND FOR FRYING

1 MEDIUM AUBERGINE, ABOUT 700G

1 LARGE EGG

1 LARGE GARLIC CLOVE, FINELY CHOPPED

2 TABLESPOONS FINELY CHOPPED FRESH FLAT-LEAF PARSLEY

1 TEASPOON FINELY CHOPPED FRESH MARJORAM, OR ½ TEASPOON DRIED MARJORAM

SEA SALT, TO TASTE

FRESHLY GROUND BLACK PEPPER

10G BREADCRUMBS, PLUS 50G FOR DREDGING

1. Preheat the oven to 200°C/400°F/gas mark 6.

2. Lightly oil a baking tray with olive oil. Slice the aubergine in half lengthways. Place each half cut side down on the tray. Roast until soft, about 30 minutes. Remove from the oven and leave to cool. Use a spoon to scoop excess seeds out of the aubergine; discard them. Scoop the flesh of the aubergine out of the skin and squeeze it to get rid of as much liquid as you can; finely chop and place in a colander to drain until you are ready to combine it with the other ingredients.

3. In a mixing bowl, beat the egg with the garlic, parsley, marjoram, 1 teaspoon salt and pepper to taste. Add the aubergine and the 10g breadcrumbs. Thoroughly mix all the ingredients together. Chill for 1 hour or overnight.

4. Pour olive oil in a frying pan to reach 4cm up the sides of the pan. Place over medium-high heat. Line a platter with kitchen paper. Spread the remaining breadcrumbs on a plate. Remove the aubergine mixture from the fridge and, using your hands, form small balls the size of a walnut. When the oil is sizzling hot, roll the balls in the breadcrumbs. Press to flatten into a cookie shape and slip them into the hot oil one at a time. Fry until crispy and golden, about 5 minutes in all, turning them over midway through cooking. Use a skimmer to transfer them to kitchen paper. Sprinkle lightly with salt immediately. Cook all the fritters in this fashion. Serve hot.

COURGETTE
FRITTERS
Serves 4

At least half the weight of courgettes is water, which can make many courgette dishes sodden. But these fritters are very light and delicate as a result of salting and draining the shredded raw courgettes prior to forming the batter. I can hardly get the tasty morsels from cooker to table before little hands snatch them as quickly as they are fried.

900G SMALL COURGETTES, EACH WEIGHING BETWEEN 175 AND 225G

2 TEASPOONS SEA SALT, PLUS MORE FOR SPRINKLING

2 LARGE EGGS, BEATEN

3 TABLESPOONS FRESHLY GRATED AGED GENIUNE ASIAGO, PARMIGIANO-REGGIANO OR GRANA PADANO

1 TABLESPOON PLAIN UNBLEACHED WHITE FLOUR

1 TABLESPOON FINE BREADCRUMBS

FRESHLY GROUND BLACK PEPPER

PURE OLIVE OIL, FOR FRYING

1. Wash the courgettes well and slice off the stem and navel. Grate them on the large holes of a box grater or with a shredding attachment in a food-processor. Put the courgettes in a colander and sprinkle with 2 teaspoons salt. Place a plate on top. Over the plate, place a heavy weight such as a kettle filled with water or a very large tin of food. Put the colander in the sink positioned over the plughole. Allow the courgettes to release their water for at least an hour or up to two hours. Transfer the shredded courgette to a clean tea towel to blot the remaining moisture, then place it in a mixing bowl, first using your hands to wring as much liquid out of the courgette as possible.

2. Combine the shredded courgette, eggs, cheese, flour, breadcrumbs and pepper. The mixture should be soft but not watery; if it is too thick, the fritters will be heavy. Chill the mixture for an hour or up to two hours.

3. Pour enough olive oil in a frying pan to come 4cm up the sides. Turn on the heat and when the oil is sizzling hot, slip the courgette mixture in one rounded teaspoon at a time. Take care not to crowd the pan; the fritters need plenty of room to cook. Fry until golden and crisp, about 5 minutes in total, turning them over when they are golden brown on one side. Use a skimmer or tongs to transfer the fritters to kitchen paper to drain. Sprinkle with sea salt as soon as they are taken out of the oil. Repeat this procedure with the remaining batter. Serve the fritters at once.

NICK GUALANO'S
SAVOURY SUMMER SQUASH PANCAKES
Serves 4

Called *pizze fritte* in Calabria, these savoury pancakes, which I learned from my neighbour's son, Chef Nick Gualano, are popular during the summer and autumn harvest when courgettes are profuse in the garden. They can be made with small courgettes (fewer seeds, less water content and more flavour) or with courgette flowers. If using courgette flowers, first remove the stem and stamen, and slice the flower into ribbons; there is no need to salt and drain them first as for the squash. *Pizze fritte* are excellent for lunch or a light dinner, and they are best eaten hot as soon as they are made. Use the courgette flowers on the day you pick them or buy them. Wrap them loosely in damp kitchen paper and chill them until ready to cook.

225G COURGETTES OR YELLOW SUMMER SQUASH

2 TEASPOONS SEA SALT, PLUS MORE FOR SPRINKLING

2 LARGE EGGS

3 LARGE GARLIC CLOVES, FINELY CHOPPED

¼ TEASPOON FRESHLY GROUND BLACK PEPPER

50G FRESHLY *GRATED* PARMIGIANO-REGGIANO, PECORINO ROMANO OR GRANA PADANO CHEESE

30G UNBLEACHED PLAIN FLOUR

OLIVE OIL, FOR FRYING

1. Grate the squash on the coarse side of a box grater, or shred it using the shredding attachment of a food processor; transfer it to a colander. Toss with 1 teaspoon of the salt. Put the colander in a sink and place a plate and heavy weight such as a large, filled tin on top. Allow the liquid to drain, about 30 minutes. Using your hands, squeeze as much liquid from the squash as you can.

2. Beat the eggs and add the garlic, the other teaspoon of salt, pepper and grated cheese. Whisk in the flour. Fold in the squash.

3. Warm 3 tablespoons of the olive oil over medium heat in an ample frying pan. Drop 2 tablespoons of the squash batter in the pan to form small pancakes. Fry until golden on both sides, about 4 minutes. Transfer to a serving dish. Sprinkle salt on the pancakes as soon as they come out of the pan. Serve at once.

CHAPTER

2

EVERYDAY SAUCES AND DRESSINGS

When I once asked a cousin how he'd found the food in France, he replied, 'I don't know. There was so much sauce on everything I couldn't tell.' The Italian way with sauces (and dressings) is different. For most meats and fish, the natural juices suffice when fortified with wine, vinegar, lemon or herbs. Olive oil alone, before cooking or after, brings out the flavours of many simple dishes. Most important are the tomato and meat sauces for pasta and polenta, as in the Neapolitan saying, *Criste mì, fa chiove le maccarrune, e le chianghe de le logge fatta ragù;* 'Sweet Jesus, make it rain macaroni, and turn our balconies into pots of ragù.' One of the most comforting rituals of Sundays and holidays is the rite of their preparation, which begins early in the morning. Mother or grandmother is up long before the rest of the household, gently clanging her pots and pans, a clatter far kinder to the sleepy ear than any raucous alarm clock. To Italian cooks, sauces are like reflexes, even instincts, and there is no one standard or 'best' recipe for any of them. Here are the ones I turn to time and time again.

FRUITY NEAPOLITAN TOMATO SAUCE
('POMAROLA')

Makes about 450ml

I learned to make *Pomarola,* or *pummarola* in dialect, a traditional sauce for spaghetti and macaroni, from my aunt, who lived in Naples for much of her life. It consists of fresh tomatoes in season, or tinned tomatoes. Because it begins with a generous *battuto* (a vegetable base), it is fruity and fragrant and has a great deal of texture. It is well suited to the texture of dried pasta; linguine and bucatini are especially compatible with it, and this recipe is enough for 450g of it. When sieved, *pomarola* can be used as a foundation for other sauces or ragù.

500G TINNED, PEELED PLUM TOMATOES IN JUICE, OR 1.1KG FRESH, SWEET, MATURE VINE-RIPENED PLUM TOMATOES, PEELED, DESEEDED AND CHOPPED (SEE STEP 1)

4 TABLESPOONS EXTRA-VIRGIN OLIVE OIL

2 LARGE GARLIC CLOVES, CRUSHED

1 SMALL RED ONION, FINELY CHOPPED

1 MEDIUM CELERY STICK, INCLUDING LEAVES, FINELY CHOPPED

1 SMALL CARROT, FINELY CHOPPED

2 TABLESPOONS FRESH FLAT-LEAF PARSLEY, FINELY CHOPPED

SMALL HANDFUL OF CHOPPED FRESH BASIL

2 TABLESPOONS TOMATO PURÉE

½ TEASPOON SALT, OR TO TASTE

FRESHLY GROUND BLACK OR WHITE PEPPER

1. If using tinned tomatoes, drain them and reserve their juice; chop and set aside. If using fresh tomatoes, bring a large saucepan three-quarters full of water to the boil. Blanch the tomatoes for 30 to 45 seconds; drain and plunge into cold water. Using a paring knife, lift off the skins and cut out the tough area around the core. Cut the tomatoes into quarters lengthways, push out excess seeds and chop.

2. In a saucepan over medium-low heat, warm 3 tablespoons of the olive oil. Stir in the garlic, onion, celery, carrot, parsley and basil, and sauté until completely soft, about 12 minutes. Add the tomato purée and sauté for 3 minutes. Then add the tomatoes and their juice, cover partially and simmer gently until thickened, about 45 minutes. Season to taste. Remove from the heat and stir in the remaining 1 tablespoon olive oil before serving.

NOTE: To make a smooth sauce, leave to cool and then pass through a food mill over a saucepan, pressing out as much pulp as possible. Place over medium heat just to heat through, about 3 minutes. Remove from the heat and stir in the remaining olive oil.

AHEAD-OF-TIME NOTE: The sauce can be made 4 to 5 days ahead of time and stored tightly covered in the refrigerator, or it can be frozen for up to 3 months. Leave out the remaining 1 tablespoon olive oil and stir it into the sauce after reheating.

LONG-SIMMERED
BOLOGNESE MEAT SAUCE

Makes about 450ml

Salsa Bolognese, also known as *ragù bolognese,* has travelled far and wide outside the borders of Bologna, and no wonder. This complex, fragrant and delicate meat sauce, versions of which simmer in pots all over the region of Emilia-Romagna in preparation for midday Sunday lunch, is one of the marvels of the Italian table. While I have listed minced beef in this recipe, a combination of veal, pork and beef can be used for an even more complex sauce. *Salsa Bolognese* is typically used between layers of homemade lasagne in Bologna's region, and it is the classic sauce for homemade tagliatelle. Pappardelle and fettuccine are also suitable matches. The most compatible macaroni cuts are fusilli corti (short twists), gnocchetti and rigatoni. Pass freshly grated Parmigiano-Reggiano at the table.

550G TINNED, PEELED PLUM TOMATOES IN JUICE

3 TABLESPOONS UNSALTED BUTTER

1 TABLESPOON EXTRA-VIRGIN OLIVE OIL

1 SMALL WHITE OR YELLOW ONION, FINELY CHOPPED

1 SMALL CELERY STICK, INCLUDING LEAVES, FINELY CHOPPED

½ SMALL CARROT, SCRAPED AND FINELY CHOPPED

1 TABLESPOON CHOPPED FRESH FLAT-LEAF PARSLEY

350G LEAN MINCED BEEF, PREFERABLY BRAISING STEAK

½ TEASPOON SALT, OR TO TASTE

125ML GOOD-QUALITY DRY WHITE WINE

150ML MILK

⅛ TEASPOON NUTMEG, PREFERABLY FRESHLY GRATED

FRESHLY GROUND WHITE OR BLACK PEPPER

TASTY MEAT STOCK, AS NEEDED (PAGE 213)

450G PASTA, COOKED, TO SERVE 4

1. Drain the tomatoes, reserving their juice. Chop and set aside.

2. In a large, wide cast-iron casserole dish or large, deep frying pan over low heat, melt 2 tablespoons of the butter with the olive oil. Stir in the onion, celery, carrot and parsley and sauté until soft but not at all browned, about 12 minutes. Keeping the heat very low, add the minced meat. The meat must heat very gently, only enough to colour it lightly on the outside; allowing it to absorb the flavours of the other ingredients and to become delicate and creamy. Stir in the salt and wine. Simmer very gently for several minutes until the the liquid is absorbed.

3. Add the milk and nutmeg. (It is important to add the milk before adding the tomatoes so that it is absorbed by the meat.) Simmer gently for 10 minutes, then add the tomatoes and juice. As soon as the sauce begins to simmer, turn the heat down to the lowest setting. Cover partially and simmer, stirring occasionally, for about 4 hours. If the sauce begins to dry out, stir in a small amount of the meat

stock a little at a time. Stir in the remaining butter and pepper and check for seasoning. Serve over the cooked pasta.

AHEAD-OF-TIME NOTE: This sauce can be made 3 or 4 days in advance and stored tightly covered in the fridge or it can be frozen for up to 3 months. Leave out the remaining 1 tablespoon butter and the pepper. Stir them in after reheating the sauce.

20-MINUTE TOMATO SAUCE
WITH GARLIC

Makes about 500ml

This is a homey, quick and chunky tomato sauce, rustic in character due to its texture and to the large quantity of garlic. I often use it for dried pasta dishes, or on freshly made gnocchi or ravioli.

550G TINNED, PEELED PLUM TOMATOES IN JUICE

3 TABLESPOONS EXTRA-VIRGIN OLIVE OIL

4 LARGE GARLIC CLOVES, SMASHED

2 TABLESPOONS TOMATO PURÉE

2 OR 3 FRESH BASIL LEAVES

¼ TEASPOON SALT, OR TO TASTE

FRESHLY GROUND BLACK PEPPER

1. Drain the tomatoes, reserving their juice. Using your hands or a potato masher, crush the tomatoes well. Set aside.

2. In a cold saucepan over medium-low heat, warm 2 tablespoons of the olive oil and the garlic together, and sauté until the garlic is soft but not coloured, 3 to 4 minutes. Add the tomato purée and stir; then add the tomatoes and their strained juice. Simmer over low heat, uncovered, until enough of the liquid evaporates to form a sauce that will coat a spoon, about 25 minutes. Tear the basil into small pieces and stir them into the sauce along with the salt. Simmer for another minute or two. Remove from the heat and stir in the pepper and the remaining 1 tablespoon olive oil.

VARIATION: Substitute 1 small red, white or yellow onion, chopped, for the garlic.

AHEAD-OF-TIME NOTE: The sauce can be made 4 to 5 days in advance of using and stored tightly covered in the fridge, or it can be frozen for up to 3 months. Whether storing it in the fridge or freezer, leave out the basil, pepper and last tablespoon olive oil. Stir them into the sauce after reheating.

TOMATO SAUCE WITH BACON AND SAFFRON

Makes about 700ml

It is characteristic of Sardinian cooking to add saffron to sauces, as in this recipe, which I learned to make from my aunt, Rita Ghisu. Not only does saffron impart an incomparable and beguiling flavour, it gives the sauce a beautiful, deep golden cast. The back bacon enriches its flavour, but is removed after sautéing; the crispy lardons are reserved for scattering on top before serving. This sauce is traditionally served with *malloreddus,* a pasta peculiar to the island. Cavatelli or conchiglie ('shells') are the closest substitutes. Pass freshly grated young (mild) Pecorino, Parmigiano-Reggiano or Grana Padano at the table with the sauce.

550G TINNED, PEELED PLUM TOMATOES IN JUICE

3 TABLESPOONS EXTRA-VIRGIN OLIVE OIL

50G BACK BACON, THICK-SLICED AND CUT INTO MATCHSTICK STRIPS (LARDONS)

4 LARGE GARLIC CLOVES, BRUISED

2 TABLESPOONS TOMATO PURÉE

2 ENVELOPES (⅛ TEASPOON TOTAL) SAFFRON POWDER, OR ⅛ TEASPOON SAFFRON THREADS

SALT

4 FRESH BASIL LEAVES

450G PASTA, COOKED, TO SERVE 4

1. Drain the tomatoes, reserving their juice. Chop the tomatoes and set aside.

2. In a saucepan over low heat, warm the olive oil. Add the back bacon and sauté gently until it is coloured nicely and crispy, about 2 minutes. Set aside. Increase the heat to medium-low, add the garlic, and sauté until lightly coloured, about 8 minutes. Add the chopped tomatoes and their juice and simmer over medium-low heat until excess liquid from the tomatoes has evaporated, about 10 minutes. Stir in the tomato purée. If using saffron threads, dissolve them in a tablespoon of hot water and stir them into the sauce. If using saffron powder, simply stir it into the sauce. Season with salt and simmer gently, uncovered, over medium-low heat, until a thick consistency forms, about 30 minutes. Stir the sauce occasionally as it cooks.

3. Stir in the basil during the last 20 minutes of cooking. Taste and adjust the salt.

4. Toss with the hot pasta. Sprinkle each serving plate with some of the reserved crispy lardons.

AHEAD-OF-TIME NOTE: This sauce can be made 4 or 5 days in advance and stored tightly covered in the fridge, or it can be frozen for up to 3 months. Leave out the basil until you reheat the sauce.

SOUTHERN-STYLE
BEEF AND PORK RAGÙ
Makes about 560ml

Variations of this dense, richly flavoured sauce are part of the landscape in kitchens all across the *Mezzogiorno,* as the southern regions of Italy are called. Making it is so much a part of local folklore that it has been the subject of vernacular poetry, song and street theatre. Its aroma is part of the fabric of my own childhood memories. This is how my mother made it. Use this sauce for spaghetti, or for macaroni cuts such as rigatoni, ziti, penne or cavatelli.

675G TINNED, PEELED PLUM TOMATOES IN JUICE

450G BRAISING STEAK, IN ONE PIECE

225G PORK SHOULDER, IN ONE PIECE, OR 1 LARGE PORK CHOP WITH BONE

3 TABLESPOONS EXTRA-VIRGIN OLIVE OIL

2 LARGE GARLIC CLOVES, CRUSHED

1 MEDIUM RED ONION, FINELY CHOPPED

1 SMALL CARROT, FINELY CHOPPED

1 SMALL CELERY STALK, FINELY CHOPPED

110G TOMATO PURÉE

125ML GOOD-QUALITY DRY RED WINE

SALT AND FRESHLY GROUND BLACK PEPPER

175ML WATER

1 TEASPOON CHOPPED FRESH BASIL

450G PASTA, COOKED, TO SERVE 4

1. Drain the tomatoes, reserving their juice. Chop and set aside. Trim excess fat from the steak and pork, but leave each of the meats in one piece.

2. In a cast-iron casserole dish over medium-high heat, warm the olive oil and brown the meats on all sides, about 12 minutes. Transfer to a dish and set aside. Reduce the heat to medium-low, add the garlic, onion, carrot and celery, and sauté until softened, about 10 minutes. Stir in the tomato purée and sauté for 3 minutes.

3. Return the meat with any juices to the pan and add the wine. Simmer, uncovered, until the liquid evaporates, about 3 minutes. Add the tomatoes and their juice and season with salt and pepper. Stir in the water and basil and bring to the boil. Reduce the heat to low, cover partially and simmer, stirring occasionally, until the meat is tender and the sauce has thickened, about 1 hour and 45 minutes.

4. When the sauce is done, remove the meat and slice. Serve the sauce over pasta and the meat on a side dish. For a smooth sauce, cut the meat into dice and pass it together with the sauce through a food mill. A food-processor will make a slightly thicker sauce, since it doesn't actually strain any part of it.

AHEAD-OF-TIME NOTE: This sauce can be made 3 or 4 days in advance and stored tightly covered in the refrigerator, or it can be frozen for up to 3 months.

MUSHROOM RAGÙ

Makes about 560ml

Because my children were vegetarians throughout their childhoods, I created alternatives to the wonderful meat ragù that often bubbled on my hob and would seduce them. Here is one of the meatless sauces I created. The combination of dried porcini mushrooms and wild mushrooms give it astonishing flavour. As with all these sauce recipes, this is enough for 450g of pasta and can be paired with virtually all cuts that are appropriate for saucing. It can also be used as a side sauce with eggs or as a topping for polenta or simple rice dishes.

10G DRIED PORCINI MUSHROOMS

225G FRESH MUSHROOMS, INCLUDING SHIITAKE, OYSTER OR CHANTERELLE

3 TABLESPOONS EXTRA-VIRGIN OLIVE OIL

2 TABLESPOONS UNSALTED BUTTER

4 LARGE GARLIC CLOVES, SLICED

1 SMALL ONION, CHOPPED

2 TEASPOONS FINELY CHOPPED FRESH ROSEMARY, OR 1 TABLESPOON DRIED CRUMBLED ROSEMARY

3 TABLESPOONS TOMATO PURÉE

125ML GOOD-QUALITY DRY RED WINE

250ML TASTY MEAT STOCK (PAGE 213)

SALT AND FRESHLY GROUND BLACK PEPPER

1. Prepare the dried and fresh mushrooms: Soak the dried porcini in a small bowl with 250ml hot water for 15 to 20 minutes. Use a slotted spoon to lift them out; rinse under cold running water to remove any sand or grit. Squeeze out the excess water and give them a rough chop. Strain the soaking liquid through muslin or a kitchen paper-lined sieve to remove any grit. Set aside the mushrooms and the strained liquid separately. With a clean tea towel, wipe any dirt from the fresh mushrooms. Cut off any woody stem tips and slice them thin.

2. In a deep, non-stick frying pan, combine the olive oil, butter and garlic. Sauté gently until the garlic softens, about 1 minute. Stir in the onion and rosemary and sauté for another minute. Add the porcini and other mushrooms and sauté over medium heat until they sweat, about 5 minutes, tossing frequently.

3. Dilute the tomato purée in the reserved mushroom soaking liquid and add to the sauce. Stir in the wine. Simmer over medium-low heat until the liquid evaporates, about 1 minute. Pour in the stock and continue to simmer, until the flavours marry, about 10 minutes. Season with salt and pepper.

AHEAD-OF-TIME NOTE: This sauce can be made 3 or 4 days in advance of using and stored tightly covered in the fridge, or it can be frozen for up to 3 months.

VIOLA BUITONI'S LONG-SIMMERED
TOMATO SAUCE with RIBS and SAUSAGES

Serves 4 to 6

In the early 1950s, Buitoni was a household word in my Italian family, transplanted in a new land where authentic ingredients were hard to come by. Many years later, I met Viola, the daughter of Buitoni pasta company founder Paolo Buitoni. She had an elite catering company in New York City and eventually opened her own speciality Italian food shop. This is one of her family recipes, a thick, succulent stew swimming with pork ribs and sweet sausage. Serve it with polenta (see page 217) or pasta.

5 TABLESPOONS EXTRA-VIRGIN OLIVE OIL

18 BABY BACK RIBS, OR 1.8KG 'COUNTRY-STYLE' PORK RIBS (BONE-IN RIB ENDS), CUT OFF THE RACK INTO INDIVIDUAL RIBS

9 ITALIAN PORK SAUSAGES

1 ONION, FINELY CHOPPED

1 CARROT, FINELY CHOPPED

3 CELERY STICKS WITH LEAVES, FINELY CHOPPED

3 WHOLE ROSEMARY SPRIGS, LEAVES REMOVED AND FINELY CHOPPED, OR 1 TEASPOON CRUMBLED DRIED ROSEMARY

125ML DRY RED WINE

1.6KG TINNED ITALIAN PLUM TOMATOES, DRAINED (RESERVE JUICES), DESEEDED AND CHOPPED

SEA SALT

1. In a large, heavy-bottomed wide cast-iron casserole dish, warm the olive oil over medium heat. Add the ribs and sausages, separating the links if they are attached. Sauté over medium-low to medium heat until lightly browned all over, about 25 minutes. Transfer the meat to a side dish and add the onion, carrot, celery and rosemary to the pan. Reduce the heat to medium-low; sauté, stirring occasionally, until the vegetables are well softened, about 10 minutes.

2. Return the ribs and sausages to the pan and toss all together. Pour in the wine and stir to distribute well. Cook to evaporate the liquid, about 3 minutes. Add the tomatoes and their juice, cover and simmer, stirring occasionally, until the sauce is thick and the meat is so tender it actually falls off the bones, 2½ to 3 hours. Remove from the heat, taste for salt and serve.

BLANCHED BASIL PESTO
(FOOD PROCESSOR METHOD)

Makes 340g

In summer there is always plenty of basil growing in my garden. My daughter forever tends it and prunes its sprigs, and delivers baskets of it for me to make one of her favourite sauces, *pesto alla genovese*. This recipe differs from others I've published in that the basil is blanched before using. While this is a departure from the classic method, blanching prevents the basil from turning brown and surprisingly doesn't interfere with its flavour or texture. Pesto needs a sturdy pasta to support it – fettuccine, nidi, spaghetti, bucatini or linguine.

1 TABLESPOON KOSHER SALT

40G FRESH BASIL LEAVES, SOLIDLY PACKED 2 GARLIC CLOVES, CUT INTO PIECES

35G LIGHTLY TOASTED PINE NUTS

GENEROUS ½ TEASPOON SALT

FRESHLY GROUND BLACK PEPPER

125ML EXTRA-VIRGIN OLIVE OIL

50G FRESHLY GRATED PARMIGIANO-REGGIANO CHEESE

2 TABLESPOONS UNSALTED BUTTER, SOFTENED TO ROOM TEMPERATURE

450G PASTA, COOKED, TO SERVE 4

1. In a saucepan, bring 950ml water to the boil and add the kosher salt and basil leaves. Press the basil with a skimmer to keep it submerged for 30 seconds. Drain immediately and shock it in an ice-water bath to stop the cooking. Squeeze the basil leaves with your hands to remove excess water. Coarsely chop.

2. Put the basil, garlic, pine nuts, salt, a few grinds of pepper and the oil into the bowl of a food-processor. Blend to a smooth purée, stopping the machine once or twice to scrape the sides of the container. Add the grated cheeses and butter, and blend for about 15 seconds. Scrape the sides again and blend for another few seconds. Do not overdo, or your pesto will have very little texture.

3. When cooking your pasta, save some of the cooking water and stir 1 tablespoon of it with the pesto before combining it with steaming hot pasta; use another few tablespoons or so to moisten the pasta when you toss the pesto with it.

NOTE: For a pesto with better texture, leave the grated cheese and butter out and beat them in by hand when you have finished blending the other ingredients.

KEEPING PESTO: Pesto will keep in the fridge for several months after transferring to a sterilised sealed glass jar. Push a layer of clingfilm on the surface of the pesto. This is far more effective than the traditional method of pouring olive oil on the surface. Leave out the salt, cheese and butter and beat them in just before using.

FRESH
TOMATO VINAIGRETTE

Makes 250ml

This appealing tomato-coloured dressing is best to make when a luscious and sweet freshly picked garden tomato is at hand. Toss it with leafy salads or cooked vegetable salads.

1 SWEET, VINE-RIPENED TOMATO

1 LARGE SHALLOT, FINELY CHOPPED

1 TEASPOON DIJON MUSTARD

FINELY CHOPPED FRESH FLAT-LEAF
PARSLEY

SEA SALT AND FRESHLY GROUND BLACK
OR WHITE PEPPER

60ML GOOD-QUALITY WHITE WINE
VINEGAR OR SHERRY VINEGAR

175ML OLIVE OIL

1. Cut the tomato in half and push out the seeds. Squeeze out excess juices and chop.

2. Combine the shallot, mustard, parsley, salt and pepper to taste and vinegar and allow to macerate for up to an hour, if you have the time.

3. Stir in the olive oil and tomato and whizz in a food-processor; pulse for a few seconds more. Taste for seasoning.

WINE, CAPER AND SHALLOT DRESSING

Makes 180ml

An alternative to vinegary dressings that interfere with tasting your wine when eating salad, this dressing uses wine instead of vinegar. Use a red wine that you can drink with your meal.

1 LARGE SHALLOT, FINELY CHOPPED

2 TABLESPOONS DIJON MUSTARD

2 TABLESPOONS FINELY CHOPPED
FRESH FLAT-LEAF PARSLEY

SEA SALT AND FRESHLY GROUND BLACK
OR WHITE PEPPER

2 TEASPOONS ANCHOVY PASTE

2 TABLESPOONS CHOPPED CAPERS

60ML GOOD-QUALITY FULL-BODIED
DRY RED WINE

125ML OLIVE OIL

1. Combine the shallot, mustard, parsley, sea salt, pepper to taste, anchovy paste, capers and wine and allow to macerate for up to an hour, if you have the time.

2. Stir in the olive oil. Taste and adjust the salt if necessary.

CHAPTER

3

TO YOUR HEALTH:
SIDE SALADS AND MAIN SALADS

The map shows why Italians love vegetables: All those mountains! So little farmland! (And even the steepest slopes have been laboriously terraced for a few extra acres to cultivate.) From childhood, vegetables have been treats to Italians. Green leaves, tomatoes and a shower of shredded carrots, and perhaps some field greens, aid digestion and clear the palate; but they are more important for their link to the family and the land. There is variety in plenty: tender lettuces, bitter chicory or bold radicchio for accents; beet greens for colour and health; rocket for bite. Elaborate salads include asparagus or courgettes, rice, potatoes, grains, beans, eggs, meat and seafood. (But never pasta. In Italy, pasta is served hot and eaten immediately. Don't wait for everyone to be served.) Salads are appetisers or side dishes; and they may replace hot meals in summer or join the mosaic of the antipasto table. Olive oil – seductive or assertive – and wine vinegar or lemon juice are musts for most dressings, although, for a few salads, nothing will do but fresh mayonnaise (see page 218). Here is an assortment of salads for an informal meal, the buffet table or a portable feast.

RICE AND PRAWN SALAD
WITH PINE NUTS

Serves 4

While pasta is never served hot on the Italian table, rice can be prepared hot or cold, as it retains its firm texture even when marinated in an acidic dressing. This is one of the rice salads I make in summer. Short-grain rice is starchy and heavy – not characteristics we want in a salad. If you toast the rice before cooking, the grains will remain separate and firm. In addition, rinsing it well under cold running water after cooking removes excess starch, giving the rice definition in combination with the other ingredients.

220G MEDIUM-GRAIN RICE

KOSHER SALT

60ML WHITE WINE VINEGAR

450G RAW MEDIUM PRAWNS, IN THEIR SHELLS

1 WHOLE HOT RED PEPPER, DESEEDED

35G TOASTED PINE NUTS

6 TABLESPOONS FINELY CHOPPED FRESH FLAT-LEAF PARSLEY

2 TABLESPOONS FRESH BASIL, FINELY CHOPPED

FOR THE DRESSING

JUICE OF 1 LEMON, OR TO TASTE

1 SHALLOT, FINELY CHOPPED

SEA SALT

125ML EXTRA-VIRGIN OLIVE OIL, OR TO TASTE

1. Preheat an oven to 180°C/350°F/gas mark 4. Spread the rice out on a baking tray. Slide it on the middle rack of the oven to toast, 3 to 4 minutes. Leave to cool.

2. In the meantime, in a large pot, bring to a boil enough water to cover the prawns. Add 3 teaspoons salt and the vinegar. Drop in the prawns and the hot red pepper and cover. Bring to the boil over high heat, stirring occasionally, until the prawns are just cooked through, about 3 minutes. They should be pink on the surface and opaque inside. Drain, reserving the cooking water but discard the pepper. Cool and then shell, removing the tails.

3. Strain the prawn stock. Add enough water to make 3.8 litres. Bring it to the boil and stir in the rice and 1 tablespoon salt. Boil until tender but firm to the bite, about 15 minutes, depending on the rice. Rinse immediately in cold running water until it runs clear. Drain well and spread out on a clean tea towel to dry.

4. In a salad bowl, make the dressing: Combine the lemon juice, shallot and sea salt to taste. Whisk in the olive oil in a slow stream. Add the rice, prawns, pine nuts, parsley and basil. Check for seasoning and serve at once.

AHEAD-OF-TIME NOTE: The salad can be made 3 hours in advance. It is best if it is not refrigerated before serving. The lemon juice should be added just before serving.

PUGLIESE RICE SALAD
WITH MANY PICKLED VEGETABLES

Serves 8 to 10

My Roman-born friend Anna Maria Erenbourg Weld spends her summers in Puglia, where she learned how to make this exceptional, complex and tangy rice salad filled with the region's celebrated pickled vegetables, *sott'aceti* in Italian. It is typically made in a large quantity for big family gatherings because the terrific variety of ingredients it contains makes it impractical for a small batch. Consider it for entertaining or special occasions when expecting a large gathering. Success will depend largely on the quality of the pickled vegetables and other ingredients you use. The best are genuine Italian mixed *sott'aceti* imported from Italy. See Rice and Prawn Salad (page 48) for notes on selecting and cooking rice for salads.

450G MEDIUM-GRAIN RICE

2 TABLESPOONS KOSHER SALT

1 LEMON, SLICED IN HALF

450G CACIOCAVALLO, OR FRESH MOZZARELLA, DICED

90G GAETA OLIVES, RINSED, PITTED AND HALVED

80G PICKLED AUBERGINE, DRAINED

90G TINY PICKLED ONIONS, DRAINED

80G MIXED ITALIAN PICKLED VEGETABLES, DRAINED

80G PICKLED ROASTED ARTICHOKES

80G PORCINI MUSHROOMS PRESERVED IN OLIVE OIL, DRAINED

80G PICKLED ROASTED PEPPERS, DRAINED

60G CAPERS, DRAINED

150G SWEET, VINE-RIPENED CHERRY TOMATOES, HALVED

6 HARD-BOILED EGGS, SLICED

3 200-G TINS ITALIAN TUNA PRESERVED IN OLIVE OIL, DRAINED AND FLAKED

5 TABLESPOONS CHOPPED FRESH MINT

EXTRA-VIRGIN OLIVE OIL, TO TASTE

YELLOW MUSTARD, TO TASTE

SEA SALT AND FRESHLY GROUND BLACK PEPPER

220G HOMEMADE MAYONNAISE (PAGE 218)

1. Preheat the oven to 180°C/350°F/gas mark 4. Spread the rice out on a baking tray. Slide it on the middle rack of the oven to toast, 3 to 4 minutes. Leave to cool.

2. In a large saucepan, bring 4.7 litres of water to a rapid boil. Add the salt and lemon halves. Boil until the rice is cooked but firm to the bite, about 15 minutes. Drain at once and rinse thoroughly in cold running water until it runs clear. Drain again. Spread the rice out on a clean tea towel to dry.

3. In an ample serving bowl, combine the cooked rice with all the other ingredients. Toss well and serve.

AHEAD-OF-TIME NOTE: You may prepare the rice salad several hours in advance.

WARM SALT COD and POTATO SALAD

Serves 4 to 6

I love the un-fishy flavour and chewy texture of salt cod, *baccalà* in Italian. Like so many Italians, I grew up eating it. My mother often made it on Christian days of abstinence, but she always varied the recipe. It might have been a tomato stew specked with dry-cured black olives, a 'white' version with potatoes and green olives, or, in summer, a room-temperature salad like this one. Select the skinless and boneless variety of *baccalà,* which eliminates tedious and unnecessary preparation. Look for meaty, creamy-coloured fillets and avoid excessively thin, brown pieces. The dressing used here is also typically used for salads of freshly cooked fish fillets or boiled crabmeat. A richer alternative is Light Lemon Mayonnaise (page 218).

700G SKINLESS, BONELESS BACCALÀ

THICK APPLE SLICE OR ½ POTATO

225G POTATOES (CHOOSE A GOOD VARIETY FOR BOILING)

5 TABLESPOONS EXTRA-VIRGIN OLIVE OIL, OR TO TASTE

3 TABLESPOONS FRESHLY SQUEEZED LEMON JUICE, OR TO TASTE

1 MEDIUM GARLIC CLOVE, FINELY CHOPPED

FRESHLY GROUND BLACK PEPPER

FINE SEA SALT

3 TABLESPOONS CHOPPED FRESH FLAT-LEAF PARSLEY

1. To prepare the salt cod, place it in a bowl and add cold water to cover and the apple or potato, which helps to draw out the salt. Refrigerate overnight and refresh the water in the morning if not using until later in the day. Drain the salt cod and rinse in fresh cool water.

2. Place the cod in a pan with cold water to cover. Bring to the boil, then reduce the heat and cook gently until tender but not falling apart, 15 to 20 minutes. Taste before draining to make sure it is cooked. If it is still too hard, continue cooking it gently. If it is still too salty, cover with fresh cold water, bring to the boil again and drain and rinse under cold water. Drain well and pat dry with a cotton tea towel. Check for any skin and bones that may have been missed. Break up the fish into large flakes and transfer to a serving plate.

3. In a separate pan, place the potatoes with cold water to cover by 5cm. Bring to the boil, then reduce to medium-low and cook until tender, about 22 to 30 minutes, depending on the size of the potatoes. When cool enough to handle, peel them. Cut the potatoes in half and cut into 5-mm slices.

4. In a small bowl stir together the oil, lemon juice, garlic and pepper to taste. Drizzle over the fish and potatoes. Add salt to taste and sprinkle with the parsley. Serve at room temperature.

FAST-DAY SALAD WITH
TUNA, POTATOES, EGGS AND ASPARAGUS

Serves 4

Tinned Italian tuna fillets packed in olive oil are a marvellous product with a myriad of uses in the Italian kitchen. Called *ventresca*, it comes from the underside of the bonito tuna, which is light pink, moist and delicate in comparison to the dry white-meat albacore variety that is packed for the American market. It is a delight in composed salads such as this one. There are many variations of *antipasto di magro,* so-called because there is no meat in it. *Magro* means 'lean', a term often assigned to dishes served on Christian fast days. While the salad can be served with extra-virgin olive oil and good red wine vinegar, I find the dressing that most people like best is the Light Lemon Mayonnaise on page 218.

225G (5 SMALL) YUKON GOLD, OR OTHER BOILING POTATOES

3 EGGS

225G TENDER ASPARAGUS IN SEASON

1 TEASPOON SEA SALT

1 200-G TIN IMPORTED ITALIAN TUNA BELLY FILLETS IN OLIVE OIL, DRAINED AND ROUGHLY FLAKED

2 TABLESPOONS THINLY SLIVERED RED ONION, ABOUT 2.5CM LONG

HALF RECIPE LIGHT LEMON MAYONNAISE (PAGE 218)

1 TABLESPOON DRAINED SMALL CAPERS

1. Put the unpeeled potatoes in a pan with enough cold water to cover and bring to the boil over high heat. Immediately reduce the heat to medium and cook until tender when pierced with a sharp knife, about 20 minutes. Drain and when cool enough to handle, peel the potatoes and cut them crossways into 5-mm thick slices.

2. In the meantime, place the eggs in a saucepan with cold water to cover and bring to the boil. Cook them for a total of 15 minutes from the time they are placed on the cooker. Drain and peel while still warm so that they will slip out of their shells easily, then leave to cool before cutting crossways into 5-mm thick slices.

3. Remove the tough lower stalk of the asparagus. Fill another saucepan with water and bring to the boil. Add the salt, then the asparagus. Boil, uncovered, until tender, about 7 minutes. Drain, refresh in cold water and set aside. It is best if they are still warm when dressed.

4. In a salad bowl, preferably of clear glass, layer first the potatoes, then the tuna, onion, asparagus and eggs, spooning a little mayonnaise on each layer before arranging the next one. Spoon more mayonnaise on top and scatter on the capers. Serve within 2 hours of preparing.

GREEN BEAN AND POTATO SALAD
WITH PARSLEY AND BASIL

Serves 4

My aunt Rita's simple and lovely classic Italian summer salad is especially good with garden-fresh green beans, which should be cooked until tender for maximum sweetness and flavour. An 'al dente' texture should only be used for dried pasta cooking – not for most vegetables. For a creamy dressing, use Homemade Mayonnaise (page 218) thinned with a few tablespoons of white wine vinegar or lemon juice. Or make the vinaigrette dressing below.

450G YUKON GOLD OR OTHER BOILING POTATOES

450G FRESH YOUNG GREEN BEANS

1 TEASPOON COARSE SALT

1 RED ONION THINLY SLICED AND CHOPPED

4 TABLESPOONS CHOPPED FRESH FLAT-LEAF PARSLEY

4 TABLESPOONS FRESH BASIL CUT INTO CHIFFONADE

VINAIGRETTE DRESSING

125ML EXTRA-VIRGIN OLIVE OIL

1 TEASPOON DIJON MUSTARD

60ML WHITE WINE VINEGAR

1 TEASPOON SEA SALT

½ TEASPOON FRESHLY GROUND WHITE PEPPER

4 FRESHLY BOILED HARD-COOKED EGGS, CUT INTO QUARTERS

1. Place the potatoes in a pan with enough cold water to cover. Bring to the boil and cook over medium heat until tender. (Cooking time will vary based on the size of the potatoes, but count on at least 20 minutes.) Drain and refresh under cold water for several seconds. When cool enough to handle, peel. Cut into slices 5mm thick.

2. Trim the stems off the beans but leave the tapered tip intact. Bring enough water to cover to a rapid boil. Add the beans and salt. Cook until tender but not too soft or crunchy, 6 to 9 minutes depending on their size and freshness. Drain and run under cold water to refresh. Drain again.

3. Combine the ingredients for the vinaigrette dressing and mix well. Taste for seasoning.

4. Select an ample bowl and add 2 tablespoons of the dressing. Lay the potato slices on top. Sprinkle with the onion. Arrange the green beans and the eggs over that. Pour additional dressing to taste over the top, then scatter with the parsley and basil. Serve warm or at room temperature.

VARIATION: Add 1 fennel bulb, stalks trimmed, halved, cored and cut into 5-cm slices, to the cooking water with the green beans.

CAULIFLOWER SALAD
WITH CAPERS, SPRING ONIONS AND LEMON

Serves 6

This classic vegetable salad, piquant from the generous dressing of capers, olives and lemon, was a staple of my childhood. I have varied the way I make it over the years, sometimes adding cornichons and different herbs, but my friends and family seem always to love this version best.

1 LARGE HEAD CAULIFLOWER

1 TABLESPOON SALT

JUICE OF ½ LEMON

FOR THE DRESSING

3 TABLESPOONS DRAINED SMALL CAPERS OR COARSELY CHOPPED LARGE CAPERS

50G PITTED GAETA OLIVES, CUT INTO QUARTERS

1 BUNCH SPRING ONIONS, WHITE PART AND 2.5CM OF GREEN ONLY, THINLY SLICED

2 TABLESPOONS CHOPPED FRESH FLAT-LEAF PARSLEY

5 TABLESPOONS EXTRA-VIRGIN OLIVE OIL, OR TO TASTE

2 TABLESPOONS FRESHLY SQUEEZED LEMON JUICE, OR MORE TO TASTE

SALT AND FRESHLY GROUND BLACK PEPPER

1. Pour enough water into a saucepan to cover the cauliflower generously and bring it to the boil. Meanwhile, trim the stalks off the cauliflower and cut off the hard base and discard. Remove the core and separate the cauliflower into florets. Add the cauliflower to the boiling water along with the salt and lemon juice (the lemon juice will help the cauliflower to retain its colour). Cover, return to the boil and continue to cook until the cauliflower is tender but not mushy, 5 to 7 minutes. Take care, as cauliflower goes from undercooked to overcooked very quickly.

2. Meanwhile, in a small bowl combine all the dressing ingredients, including salt and pepper to taste. Whisk to blend.

3. When the cauliflower is cooked, drain it, immediately plunge it into cold water to stop further cooking and drain again. While it is still warm, toss it with the dressing in a salad bowl. Adjust seasoning for taste and serve.

FARRO SALAD
WITH CHERRY TOMATOES, FRESH MOZZARELLA AND HERBS

Serves 4

Farro, or emmer in English, has long been comfort food for the Italians and other people living near the Mediterranean. I like its chewy texture and nutty flavour best in salads such as this one.

200G WHOLE FARRO

2 TABLESPOONS FRESHLY SQUEEZED LEMON JUICE

75ML EXTRA-VIRGIN OLIVE OIL

SEA SALT AND FRESHLY GROUND BLACK PEPPER

50G FRESH MOZZARELLA CHEESE, DRAINED AND DICED

150G SWEET VINE-RIPENED CHERRY TOMATOES, HALVED

10G COMBINED FINELY CHOPPED FRESH BASIL, FLAT-LEAF PARSLEY, MARJORAM AND CHIVES

1. Rinse the farro in cold water and pick out any impurities. Cover with cold water and allow it to soak for 1 hour. Drain.

2. Bring 1.9 litres of water to the boil in a medium saucepan. Add the farro. Reduce the heat, cover and simmer, stirring from time to time, for 45 minutes or until the farro is tender. Remove from the heat and allow the grains to swell in the cooking water for 10 minutes, then drain.

3. While the farro is cooking, make the dressing. Whisk together the lemon juice, olive oil and salt and pepper to taste.

4. In a serving dish, combine the farro, cheese, tomatoes, herbs and dressing. Toss together and serve warm or at room temperature.

SWEET AND SOUR ROAST BEETROOT SALAD
WITH ORANGE AND MINT

Serves 4

Everyone who likes beetroot loves this dish. Its origins are in my family, but it has evolved in my own kitchen over the years. Red wine vinegar and good olive oil is a classic dressing, but I find that beetroot, with its natural sweetness, cry out for a sweet-and-sour treatment. I boil industrial-variety balsamic vinegar to a fruity, tart syrup and temper it with olive oil. The addition of oranges provides a burst of sweetness and a pleasant acidity.

10 SMALL TO MEDIUM BEETROOTS

3 NAVEL ORANGES

FOR THE DRESSING

125ML BALSAMIC VINEGAR

4 TABLESPOONS EXTRA-VIRGIN OLIVE OIL

1 TABLESPOON CHOPPED FRESH MINT LEAVES

1. Preheat the oven to 200°C/400°F/gas mark 6.

2. Trim the leaves off the beetroot, but do not cut into the root. Transfer to a baking tray and slide them onto the middle rack of the oven. Roast until tender, 30 to 45 minutes, depending on the freshness of the beetroot. When you can pierce them easily with a sharp knife, they are done. When they are cool enough to handle, slice off the stem stub and slip off their skins. Slice and set aside.

3. Grate the zest from one of the oranges. Using a small sharp knife, cut off the peel and white pith from all the oranges. Working over a large bowl, cut between the membranes to release the orange segments. Set aside.

4. Meanwhile, simmer the balsamic vinegar in a small pan until it is reduced to 60ml, then pass it through a small sieve to remove any sediment. Mix the olive oil and orange zest in a small bowl and stir in the reduced balsamic vinegar. In a serving bowl, arrange the beetroot and orange sections. Spoon the dressing over the salad and scatter the mint leaves on top. Serve.

AHEAD-OF-TIME NOTE: This entire dish can be prepared a day in advance with the exception of adding the mint. Cover and refrigerate. Bring to room temperature and scatter the mint on top before serving.

MY GRANDMOTHER'S
WHOLEMEAL BREAD SALAD
Serves 4

This heirloom recipe was passed down from my paternal grandmother, who learned it when her life as an immigrant was so hard and there was little else to eat besides stale bread. Despite its most humble origins, this salad is delicious. The bread must be coarse artisan bread. Other breads will not hold up to being dressed with oil and vinegar, or combined with watery tomatoes. High-quality extra-virgin olive oil is indispensable.

½ LOAF (ABOUT 450G) 2- TO 3-DAY-OLD COARSE PEASANT BREAD OR STURDY ITALIAN-STYLE BREAD, CRUSTS REMOVED

1 LARGE GARLIC CLOVE, CUT IN HALF

6 TABLESPOONS WATER, OR MORE, DEPENDING UPON THE DRYNESS OF THE BREAD

125ML EXTRA-VIRGIN OLIVE OIL

3 TABLESPOONS RED WINE VINEGAR

2 LARGE, VINE-RIPENED TOMATOES OR 4 PLUM TOMATOES, DESEEDED AND DICED, OR 310G SWEET CHERRY TOMATOES, CUT IN HALF

½ RED ONION, QUARTERED AND SLICED PAPER-THIN

2 TABLESPOONS TORN FRESH BASIL

2 TEASPOONS CHOPPED FRESH OREGANO LEAVES, OR 1 TEASPOON DRIED OREGANO

4 TABLESPOONS CHOPPED FRESH FLAT-LEAF PARSLEY

½ TEASPOON SALT, OR TO TASTE

¼ TEASPOON FRESHLY GROUND BLACK PEPPER, OR TO TASTE

1. Slice the bread and rub the slices with garlic on both sides; discard the garlic. Tear or cut the bread into 2.5-cm pieces. Place in a shallow bowl and sprinkle evenly with the 6 tablespoons of water. If the bread is very dry, you may need to add another 1 or 2 tablespoons of water.

2. In a separate bowl, stir together the olive oil, vinegar, tomatoes, onion, and half of the herbs. Leave to marinate for 10 minutes. Pour over the bread, add the remaining herbs and toss well. Season with the salt and pepper and serve.

AHEAD-OF-TIME NOTE: This salad can be made 1 or 2 hours in advance as long as a sturdy bread is used.

BREAD SALAD WITH ROASTED PEPPERS

Serves 4 to 6

The success of this salad depends on the quality of bread. It should contain no sugar, eggs or seeds and it must be chewy and substantial in order to stand up to the dressing. Three- or four-day-old sourdough or sturdy peasant bread will do nicely. Very airy, unsubstantial bread will become soggy very quickly upon contact with the dressing. Season with plenty of black pepper, a nice contrast to the sweetness of the roasted peppers.

2 LARGE RED PEPPERS, OR A COMBINATION OF RED AND YELLOW PEPPERS

450-G LOAF STURDY ITALIAN BREAD OR PEASANT BREAD

125ML EXTRA-VIRGIN OLIVE OIL

60ML WHITE WINE VINEGAR

125ML WATER

1 SMALL RED OR WHITE ONION, QUARTERED AND VERY FINELY SLICED,

1 SPRING ONION, INCLUDING 10CM OF GREEN, FINELY SLICED

2 TABLESPOONS BRINE-CURED, PITTED AND SLICED SHARPLY FLAVOURED IMPORTED GREEN OLIVES SUCH AS PICHOLINE OR SICILIAN OLIVES

1 TABLESPOON CHOPPED FRESH OREGANO OR 1 TEASPOON DRIED OREGANO

½ TEASPOON SALT

¼ TEASPOON FRESHLY GROUND BLACK PEPPER, OR MORE TO TASTE

1. First roast the peppers: arrange the peppers on a rack above a charcoal fire, or on a barbecue, or 5 to 7cm under a preheated grill, or in an oven preheated to 230°C/450°F/gas mark 8. Roast them until they are charred all over and tender inside, turning them frequently to ensure they cook evenly, about 25 minutes in the oven but less time by the other methods. Remove them from the heat. When the peppers are cool enough to handle, using a sharp knife, cut them in half vertically. Remove the stem and lift off the skin, then remove all of the seeds. Cut the peppers into 5-cm strips.

2. While the peppers are roasting, prepare the bread and the dressing. Remove all the crust from the bread and cut it into bite-size cubes. Measure out approximately four-fifths; set any excess aside for some other purpose. In a bowl, combine the oil, vinegar, water, onions, olives, herbs, salt and pepper. Allow the mixture to marinate for 10 minutes. Transfer the bread cubes and pepper strips to a salad bowl. Add the dressing and toss to unify the ingredients. Serve.

AHEAD-OF-TIME NOTE: Because the bread increasingly absorbs the dressing after the salad is made, it is best served within a few hours.

WARM WINTER GREENS SALAD
WITH BACON VINAIGRETTE

Serves 4

Like most vegetables, salad greens are seasonal in the Italian kitchen. While summer brings soft lettuces and sun-drenched tomatoes, the cool weather brings radicchio and spinach. And what better dressing for these more assertive greens than the smoky bacon, olive oil, and vinegar treatment of the Italians?

2 TABLESPOONS OLIVE OR GRAPESEED OIL

4 THICK SLICES BACON, CUT INTO 5-MM STRIPS

1 MEDIUM SHALLOT, FINELY CHOPPED

2 TABLESPOONS RED WINE VINEGAR

PINCH OF CASTER SUGAR

1 TABLESPOON DIJON MUSTARD

60ML EXTRA-VIRGIN OLIVE OIL

125G WINTER LETTUCE, SUCH AS LAMB'S LETTUCE, GEM, SPINACH OR RADICCHIO, OR A COMBINATION

SALT AND FRESHLY GROUND BLACK PEPPER

1. In an ample frying pan, warm the 2 tablespoons oil. Add the bacon and cook over medium heat until browned and crisp, about 5 minutes. Take the pan off the heat and transfer the bacon to a dish and set aside. Stir in the shallot, vinegar, sugar, mustard and extra-virgin olive oil. Using a rubber spatula to scrape it out, transfer the dressing to a large salad bowl.

2. Add the greens to the bowl and toss with the dressing. Transfer to individual serving dishes, season with salt and pepper and top with the reserved bacon. Serve at once.

COLD SEARED BEEF SALAD
WITH HERBS, CAPERS AND LEMON DRESSING

Serves 4

Leftover meat never goes to waste in my kitchen. The Italians have many inventive uses for it, exemplified in this superb family recipe for beef salad. It is so good, you need not wait for the opportunity of leftover beef to make it. I use charcoal-grilled skirt or rump steak for this salad, although care should be taken to cut the meat into very thin slices.

450G BARBECUED, ROASTED OR BOILED BEEF, TRIMMED OF FAT

FOR THE DRESSING

4 CORNICHONS, FINELY CHOPPED

1 TABLESPOON CHOPPED FRESH FLAT-LEAF PARSLEY

4 BASIL LEAVES, FINELY CHOPPED

3 TABLESPOONS DRAINED CAPERS, FINELY CHOPPED

½ TEASPOON FRESHLY GRATED LEMON ZEST

3 TABLESPOONS FRESHLY SQUEEZED LEMON JUICE

1 TEASPOON RED WINE VINEGAR

60ML EXTRA-VIRGIN OLIVE OIL

1 GENEROUS TEASPOON DIJON MUSTARD

SALT AND FRESHLY GROUND BLACK PEPPER

1. Cut the meat into thin, finger-size pieces.

2. In a small bowl combine all the dressing ingredients, including salt and pepper to taste, and, using a fork, stir to mix. Pour the dressing over the beef and toss well. Taste for seasoning. Serve at room temperature.

AHEAD-OF-TIME NOTE: The dressing can be made 4 to 5 days in advance, covered and refrigerated, then brought back to room temperature before using. Once the meat and dressing are combined, the salad can be refrigerated for several hours, or left at room temperature, covered, for 1 hour.

A BOWLFUL OF COMFORT:
SOUPS

One reason Italian food is so comforting is the custom of the long, slow meal with family and friends. Kinship and conviviality take time and besides, the most important discussions, whether about family, politics or philosophy, take place at the table. And so Italians prefer a measured procession of many plates or courses instead of the too-efficient combining of vegetable, starch and meat on a single plate. *Chi va piano va sano e lontano* ('If you go slow you get far and you get there in one piece') would be their mantra. Soup fits handily into this approach as an alternative to a pasta or risotto first course. Variety rules. A *zuppa* is weighty and chowder-like while a *minestra* is delicate, light, refined – a bit more substantial than a *brodo,* which may contain rice, tiny pasta grains or meat dumplings, or nothing at all. Then there's *minestrone* – the suffix *-one* means 'big' – thick with pasta, beans and chunked vegetables. I've tried to include at least one of each in this chapter. Soup is soothing, or should be, and so in Italy it is served warm, not hot.

RICHLY FLAVOURED CHICKEN SOUP
WITH 'PEPPERCORN' PASTINA

Serves 6

Italians believe that chicken stock 'opens the stomach' for the courses that follow during the meal. A proper chicken soup in my grandmother's kitchen consisted of clear stock made from free-range fowl from the family flock. The stock cooked for a long, slow simmer before it was strained; the idea was not to distract from its rich, clear flavour with too many vegetables or other ingredients. A handful of tiny soup pasta, a scattering of Pecorino cheese and a sprinkling of chopped parsley was the finishing touch. This recipe differs from the basic Chicken Stock on page 214 in that a whole chicken is cooked and the meat is served as a second course accompanied by a dressing, my favourite being homemade mayonnaise mixed with capers and chopped fresh herbs, or mayonnaise blended with horseradish (see page 218).

1.8KG FREE-RANGE CHICKEN

1 YELLOW ONION, UNPEELED, HALVED

1 CARROT, SCRAPED AND CUT IN HALF

1 LARGE CELERY STICK, INCLUDING LEAVES

1 LARGE FENNEL STALK, INCLUDING LEAVES (OPTIONAL)

110G PIECE CELERIAC, SLICED

1 BAY LEAF

HANDFUL OF FRESH FLAT-LEAF PARSLEY

1 TOMATO, FRESH OR TINNED

1 TABLESPOON WHOLE BLACK OR WHITE PEPPERCORNS

SEA SALT

50G ACINI DI PEPPE ('PEPPERCORN') PASTINA, OTHER SOUP PASTINA SUCH AS SEMI DI MELLONE ('MELON SEEDS'), OR ORZO ('BARLEY'), OR 110G FINE ANGEL'S HAIR PASTA

FRESHLY GRATED AGED PARMIGIANO-REGGIANO OR GRANA PADANO CHEESE, TO SERVE

1. Wash the chicken. Put all the ingredients up to but not including the salt in a 7.6-litre stockpot and cover with no more than 4cm water. Cover the pot and bring to the boil. Immediately lower to a gentle simmer and cook, partially covered, until the meat is cooked through, about 1½ hours. Skim the foam whenever it forms on the top. The stock should cook gently for the entire cooking time, never returning to the boil.

2. When the chicken is cooked, transfer to a bowl with some of the stock to keep it moist and cover. When ready to serve, remove the skin, cut the breast meat into thin slices and serve with a dressing as suggested above.

3. To make the soup, skim off as much fat from the stock as you can. Strain through a fine sieve. When ready to serve, return the stock to a clean pot, bring to the boil and add the salt and the pasta. Simmer over medium heat until al dente. Taste for seasoning. Ladle into soup bowls, sprinkle with grated cheese and serve hot.

WEDDING SOUP

Serves 10

There is much confusion about the authentic way of making Italian wedding soup because there are as many versions as there are brides. Once transported to America, home cooks put a new spin on what they cooked, making any culinary pedigree that much more removed. This is a recipe with origins in Sardinia. The little meat dumplings in the soup are called *bombetti*, 'little bombs', for their shape, but the comparison ends there. They are, in fact, very light and delicate. This is a luxurious soup, rich with tender meats and meatballs, pasta and greens.

FOR THE STOCK

1 RECIPE TASTY MEAT STOCK (PAGE 213), STRAINED

1.6KG BEEF SHORT RIBS

FOR THE BOMBETTE

1 TABLESPOON EXTRA-VIRGIN OLIVE OIL

1 ONION, FINELY CHOPPED

600G FINELY CHOPPED VEAL

110G BOILED HAM, FINELY CHOPPED

225G YUKON GOLD OR OTHER BOILING POTATOES, BOILED, PEELED AND MASHED

1 EXTRA-LARGE EGG, BEATEN

GRATED ZEST OF 1 LEMON

2 TEASPOONS FRESH FINELY CHOPPED THYME OR 1 TEASPOON DRIED THYME

2 TABLESPOONS FINELY CHOPPED FRESH FLAT-LEAF PARSLEY

25G FRESHLY GRATED PECORINO ROMANO OR PARMIGIANO-REGGIANO CHEESE

GENEROUS TWIST OF FRESHLY GROUND BLACK PEPPER

1½ TEASPOONS SEA SALT

150G FREGULA (SEE PAGE 88) OR OTHER SOUP PASTINA SUCH AS *SEMI DI MELLONE* 'MELON SEEDS'

60G SWISS CHARD, RIBS REMOVED AND CHOPPED

1. In an ample saucepan, combine the stock with the beef short ribs. Bring to the boil, then reduce to a simmer. Cook until the beef is tender and falling off the bone, about 2½ hours, skimming frequently. Cool the stock and skim off the fat.

2. Meanwhile, warm the olive oil in a medium frying pan over medium heat and sauté the onion until wilted, about 6 minutes.

3. In a bowl, combine the sautéed onion, veal, ham, mashed potatoes, egg, lemon zest, thyme, parsley, grated cheese, pepper and salt. Use your hands to mix well. Form the mixture into little oval-shaped balls about the size of pecans.

4. Bring the stock to the boil again. Add the meatballs and the fregula, if using, and simmer over medium heat, partially covered, until the pasta is 2 minutes short of cooking. If using pastina, check the packet instructions for cooking time. Add the Swiss chard and cook for 2 minutes more. Taste for seasoning and serve at once.

CLASSIC MINESTRONE

Serves 8 to 10

The secret to the success of this colourful, meatless vegetable soup is the use of fresh vegetables, high-quality extra-virgin olive oil and authentic Parmigiano-Reggiano cheese. A *battuto* (chopped mixture) of garlic, rosemary and parsley at the last minute lends extra flavour. Or stir a few tablespoons of Basil Pesto (page 44) into the soup just before serving.

3 TABLESPOONS EXTRA-VIRGIN OLIVE OIL, PLUS EXTRA TO SERVE

3 TINNED PLUM TOMATOES, DESEEDED AND FINELY CHOPPED, PLUS 60ML OF THEIR JUICES

1 LARGE ONION, COARSELY CHOPPED

1 POTATO, PEELED AND DICED

1 LARGE CELERY STICK, WITH THE LEAVES, CHOPPED

350G BUTTERNUT SQUASH, DICED

2 TEASPOONS FRESH ROSEMARY OR 1 TEASPOON DRIED ROSEMARY, PLUS 3 TABLESPOONS CHOPPED FRESH ROSEMARY OR 2 TABLESPOONS DRIED ROSEMARY

3 TABLESPOONS FINELY CHOPPED FRESH FLAT-LEAF PARSLEY LEAVES AND STEMS, PLUS ANOTHER 3 TABLESPOONS

1 LARGE CARROT, SCRAPED AND DICED

225G GREEN CABBAGE, FINELY SHREDDED

450G FRESH BORLOTTI BEANS, SHELLED OR 450G TINNED PINTO, PINK OR SMALL WHITE BEANS, RINSED AND DRAINED

2.8 LITRES WATER

2 TABLESPOONS SALT, OR TO TASTE

FRESHLY GROUND BLACK PEPPER

110G GREEN BEANS, CUT INTO 2.5CM LENGTHS

2 SMALL COURGETTES, DICED

475G CAULIFLOWER FLORETS

150G CONCHIGLIETTE ('LITTLE SHELLS') OR DITALINI ('LITTLE THIMBLES') PASTA

4 LARGE GARLIC CLOVES, FINELY CHOPPED

FRESHLY GRATED PARMIGIANO-REGGIANO CHEESE, TO SERVE

1. In a large pot, combine the olive oil, tomatoes and juice, onion, potato, celery, squash, the 2 teaspoons rosemary, the 3 tablespoons parsley, the carrot, cabbage, borlotti beans (reserve tinned beans, if using), water, salt and pepper. Cover and bring to the boil over high heat. Immediately reduce the heat to medium–low, partially cover and simmer for about 40 minutes, or until the beans are cooked.

2. Add the green beans, courgettes, cauliflower and pasta and cook for 8 minutes. Stir in the garlic, the 3 tablespoons rosemary and the 3 tablespoons parsley; if using tinned beans, add them at this point. Continue cooking the soup, uncovered, over medium heat, until the pasta is not quite al dente, about 8 minutes.

3. Serve the soup with abundant freshly grated cheese, a dribble of olive oil and a generous twist of pepper to taste.

CARROT AND FENNEL SOUP

Serves 4 to 6

Making vegetable soup without added stocks of any kind delivers the true essence of natural flavours. This is how you can do it without insipid results. If you like the flavours of carrot and fennel, that's what you'll get here, unadulterated. If you have a food-processor with a slicing attachment, you can slice the vegetables in no time at all rather than cutting them by hand. The last step – passing the puréed soup through a food mill or sieve – produces a smooth, silky texture.

1 FRESH FENNEL BULB

4 TABLESPOONS UNSALTED BUTTER OR EXTRA-VIRGIN OLIVE OIL, OR A COMBINATION

1 ONION, SLICED

700G CARROTS, SCRAPED AND SLICED INTO THIN ROUNDS

2 LITRES WATER

2 TEASPOONS SEA SALT

FRESHLY GROUND WHITE PEPPER

1. Trim the tough, dark stalks off the fennel and split the bulb in half lengthways. Cut out the tough inner core and cut the white stalks into thin slices. Chop and reserve the tender lighter green fronds.

2. In a large saucepan, warm the butter or olive oil, or a mixture of both, if using. Stir in the sliced fennel, onion and carrots and sauté over medium heat until the vegetables are softened and aromatic, about 15 minutes, stirring occasionally to prevent browning or sticking. Add the water and salt and simmer until the vegetables are completely soft, about 40 minutes. Use a hand blender to thoroughly purée the mixture. Alternatively, leave it to cool somewhat and purée it in a blender in batches.

3. For a silky texture, pass the soup through a food mill fitted with an attachment with the smallest holes. Alternatively, press the soup through a fine sieve. If you prefer a chunkier soup, serve it as is. Check for salt and add pepper to taste. Sprinkle with the chopped fennel fronds and serve.

CAULIFLOWER SOUP
WITH TINY PASTA SHELLS

Serves 6

Cauliflower, with its earthy flavour and exceptional nutritional benefits, is excellent in soups. The Italian way is to combine it with other vegetables in a nourishing, chunky potage (cream is not typically used in Italian soups). This is one of the soups I grew up on that remains a standard in my kitchen.

1 HEAD CAULIFLOWER

2 TABLESPOONS EXTRA-VIRGIN OLIVE OIL

50G LEAN PANCETTA OR SALT PORK, CUT INTO SMALL DICE

1 ONION, FINELY CHOPPED

3 CLOVES GARLIC, BRUISED

1 TEASPOON FINELY CHOPPED FRESH ROSEMARY OR ½ TEASPOON CRUSHED DRIED ROSEMARY

200G CHOPPED FRESH OR TINNED TOMATOES

1 TEASPOON SEA SALT

1.5 LITRES CHICKEN STOCK (PAGE 214), VEGETABLE STOCK (PAGE 215), OR WATER

1 MEDIUM POTATO, PEELED AND CUT INTO SMALL DICE

75G CONCHIGLIETTE (TINY PASTA SHELLS)

FRESHLY GROUND BLACK PEPPER

FRESHLY GRATED PARMIGIANO-REGGIANO, GRANA PADANO OR PECORINO *CHEESE*

1. Trim the cauliflower and remove the tough core. Separate the head into small florets.

2. In a large saucepan, warm the olive oil over medium heat and add the pancetta or salt pork. Sauté until coloured, 4 minutes. Lower the heat to medium-low and add the onion and garlic; continue to sauté until softened, 4 minutes. Add the cauliflower and rosemary; sauté an additional 5 minutes. Add the tomatoes, sea salt and stock or water. Bring to the boil. Simmer, partially covered, for 15 minutes. Add the potato and simmer for 10 minutes. Add the pasta and simmer for an additional 6 minutes. Check for salt and add pepper. Serve with grated cheese to pass round at the table.

SPICY TOMATO SOUP
WITH PANCETTA, SAFFRON AND PARMESAN CRUSTS

Serves 4

A hint I picked up from the home cooks of Parma, where Parmigiano-Reggiano cheese is made, is that the rinds of Parmigiano-Reggiano or Grana Padano cheeses have many uses, particularly in soups where they can soak and soften, resulting in scrumptious little explosions of flavour. Once you taste this soup, you will never throw out another of these cheese rinds.

1 APPROXIMATELY 5 X 7.5CM PIECE OF RIND FROM AUTHENTIC PARMIGIANO-REGGIANO OR GRANA PADANO CHEESE

3 TABLESPOONS EXTRA-VIRGIN OLIVE OIL

75G PANCETTA, CHOPPED

1 ONION, FINELY CHOPPED

2 LARGE GARLIC CLOVES, CHOPPED

10CM STRIP LEMON ZEST, ABOUT 2CM WIDE

¼ TEASPOON DRIED RED PEPPER FLAKES

1 800-G TIN CRUSHED PLUM TOMATOES

350ML CHICKEN STOCK (PAGE 214)

1 TABLESPOON FINELY CHOPPED FRESH FLAT-LEAF PARSLEY

1 TEASPOON SEA SALT

2 SACHETS PURE SAFFRON POWDER, OR ¼ TEASPOON CRUMBLED SAFFRON THREADS

1. Preheat a toaster oven to 200°C or the 'High' setting. Place the cheese rinds on the baking tray and warm them in the oven until they are easy to cut, about 5 minutes. Alternatively, zap them in a microwave oven for 20 seconds. Cut into very small dice and set aside.

2. In a large saucepan, warm the olive oil. Add the pancetta and sauté over medium heat until it is nicely browned and crisp, about 2 minutes. Use a slotted spoon to remove the pancetta from the pan and set aside. Add the onion, garlic, lemon zest and red pepper flakes to the pan and sauté over medium-low heat until softened, about 6 minutes. Stir in the crushed tomatoes, chicken stock and parsley. Simmer over medium-low heat until the mixture becomes condensed and aromatic, about 15 minutes.

3. Fish out the lemon zest and discard. Use a hand blender to roughly puree the soup. Alternatively, leave the liquid to cool somewhat and transfer it to a a blender to purée. Return to the kettle and stir in the salt and saffron. Taste for seasoning. Bring the soup to simmering point and drop in the diced cheese rinds. Turn off the heat to allow the rinds to soften. Ladle into individual soup bowls, scatter the surface with the reserved pancetta and serve.

LENTIL SOUP
WITH CRUMBLED SAUSAGE AND DITALINI PASTA

Serves 4 to 6

I have never eaten a lentil soup better than this one I grew up on. It was one of my mother's winter supper inventions, which she alternated with versions substituting smoked sausage (like *luganega,* or if she couldn't get it, Polish- or Ukrainian-style kielbasa) for fresh, sweet pork and fennel sausage.

225G BROWN LENTILS

2 LITRES CHICKEN STOCK (PAGE 214) OR WATER

1 BAY LEAF

5 LEAN, SWEET FENNEL-FLAVOURED ITALIAN PORK SAUSAGES

2 TABLESPOONS EXTRA-VIRGIN OLIVE OIL

6 LARGE GARLIC CLOVES, SMASHED

1 ONION, CHOPPED

1 LARGE CELERY STICK, INCLUDING LEAVES, CHOPPED

2 TEASPOONS FRESH THYME, FINELY CHOPPED, OR 1 TEASPOON DRIED THYME

3 TABLESPOONS TOMATO PURÉE

400-G TIN PLUM TOMATOES, PEELED, DESEEDED AND CHOPPED, LIQUID RESERVED

75G DITALINI ('LITTLE THIMBLE') PASTA

SEA SALT AND FRESHLY GROUND BLACK PEPPER

3 TABLESPOONS CHOPPED FRESH FLAT-LEAF PARSLEY

1. Pick over and wash the lentils in cold water. Transfer them to an ample saucepan, cover with the stock or water and add the bay leaf. Bring to the boil, then immediately reduce to a simmer. Cook over medium-low heat until half-cooked, 10 minutes.

2. Meanwhile, slip the casings off the sausages. In an ample frying pan, warm the olive oil. Brown the sausage meat over medium heat until lightly coloured all over, about 7 minutes. Transfer to a plate and drain any excess fat from the pan, leaving 3 tablespoons. Add the garlic, onion, celery and thyme to the pan and sauté until the garlic is golden and the vegetables are softened and aromatic, about 5 minutes. Return the sausage to the pan. Dissolve the tomato purée in a little of the lentil stock and add it to the frying pan. Follow with the chopped tomatoes and their liquid. Simmer all together for 5 minutes.

3. Bring the lentils to the boil once again if they have cooled down. Transfer the frying pan contents and the pasta to the pan with the boiling lentils. Simmer to marry the flavours, about 5 minutes. Add salt and pepper to taste. Turn off the heat, cover the pan, and leave the soup to rest until the pasta is fully cooked, about 4 more minutes. Discard the bay leaf, sprinkle with parsley, and serve.

MEATLESS PASTA AND BEAN SOUP

Serves 4 to 6

Called *pasta e fagioli* in Italian, pasta and beans are a happy union. Each is a near-perfect food in itself, composed of energising complex carbohydrates, proteins, vitamins and minerals. There are endless types of pasta and bean soups in Italy. This is one of my favourite meatless versions that I learned from my Tuscan-bred friend, Flavia Destefanis. The key to making this meatless soup flavourful is using fruity olive oil, an intensely flavoured *battuto,* or sautéed vegetable base and fresh herbs.

110G DRIED CANNELLINI BEANS, RINSED AND PICKED OVER

6 TABLESPOONS EXTRA-VIRGIN OLIVE OIL

4 LARGE GARLIC CLOVES, CRUSHED

1 ONION, CHOPPED

1 CELERY STICK, WITH LEAVES, CHOPPED

1 CARROT, CHOPPED

4 TABLESPOONS FINELY CHOPPED FLAT-LEAF PARSLEY STEMS, PLUS 3 TABLESPOONS FINELY CHOPPED LEAVES

450G VERY RIPE PLUM TOMATOES, PEELED, DESEEDED AND COARSELY CHOPPED, OR 1 450-G TIN PLUM TOMATOES, DRAINED, DESEEDED, AND COARSELY CHOPPED

1½ TEASPOONS FINELY CHOPPED FRESH ROSEMARY

2 BAY LEAVES

110G DITALINI ('LITTLE THIMBLE') PASTA

SEA SALT AND FRESHLY GROUND BLACK PEPPER

1. To rehydrate the beans, put them in an ample bowl with cold water to cover by 7.5cm. Leave to stand for 4 hours (or set aside at room temperature overnight). Alternatively, put the beans in a large saucepan with water to cover by 7.5cm. Bring to the boil, cover and remove from the heat. Let stand for 1 hour. Set aside.

2. To cook the beans, transfer them and their soaking water to an ample saucepan. Bring to the boil over high heat, then reduce the heat to medium. Cook halfway, about 30 minutes.

3. In the meantime, in a frying pan, warm the olive oil over medium heat. Stir in the garlic, onion, celery, carrot and parsley stems and sauté until the vegetables are soft and the onion transparent, about 15 minutes. Stir in the tomatoes, rosemary and bay leaves. Simmer until the tomatoes release their juices, about 10 minutes.

4. Add the frying pan contents to the pan with the beans and 950ml of water. Partially cover the pan and simmer until the beans are cooked, about 30 minutes. If the soup looks like it is drying out as it cooks, add more water. (This is a thick, hearty soup, but it should still have some stock to it.)

5. Add the pasta and 2 teaspoons salt. Simmer until the pasta is just tender, about 8 minutes. Adjust for salt and add pepper and the chopped parsley. Discard the bay leaves and serve at once.

AHEAD OF TIME NOTE: To make in advance, prepare as directed but leave out the pasta. Once made, the soup can be cooled, covered and refrigerated for up to 2 days. Cook the pasta separately in plenty of boiling salted water to cover. Drain and stir into the soup. Reheat gently and serve.

SAUSAGE AND GREENS SOUP

Serves 4

This homey soup can be made with various fresh greens, including kale, escarole, curly endive, Swiss chard or spinach. Chicken or turkey sausage can replace pork sausage, if preferred. If the stock is prepared in advance or in the freezer, the soup is quick to make.

2 TABLESPOONS EXTRA-VIRGIN OLIVE OIL

1 ONION, FINELY CHOPPED

4 SWEET ITALIAN PORK SAUSAGES (ABOUT 350G), CASINGS REMOVED

¼ TEASPOON FRESHLY GROUND FENNEL SEEDS

60G WELL-WASHED CHOPPED FRESH KALE, RIBS REMOVED, OR OTHER GREENS, STEMMED

950ML CHICKEN STOCK (PAGE 214)

110G FARFALLETTE ('TINY BUTTERFLIES') OR OTHER SMALL SOUP PASTA

SEA SALT AND FRESHLY GROUND BLACK PEPPER

FRESHLY GRATED PARMIGIANO-REGGIANO OR GRANA PADANO CHEESE

In a large saucepan, warm the olive oil over medium heat. Add the onion, sausage meat and fennel seeds and sauté until the meat is lightly coloured and the onion is soft, about 7 minutes, stirring occasionally to break up the meat. Drain off any excess fat and add the greens to the pan; sauté until wilted, 1 minute. Add the stock, bring to the boil and add the pasta. Reduce to a simmer and cook for a further 5 minutes. Taste and add salt and pepper. Serve with a generous sprinkling of grated cheese.

TUSCAN BREAD AND BEAN SOUP

Serves 4

This humble, homey soup is known as *zuppa lombarda* ('Lombard's Soup') in Tuscany, even though it has nothing to do with the northern Italian region of Lombardy. A Tuscan friend gave me the recipe years ago and it has become a standby in my family ever since. It must be made using dried, not tinned, beans because the flavourful bean-cooking liquid becomes the stock for the soup.

175G DRIED CANNELLINI BEANS

6 LARGE GARLIC CLOVES, CRUSHED

1 SPRIG FRESH SAGE WITH 8 LEAVES

3 TABLESPOONS EXTRA-VIRGIN OLIVE OIL, PLUS EXTRA FOR DRIZZLING OVER SOUP

2 TEASPOONS SEA SALT

8 SLICES STALE CIABATTA BREAD, OR OTHER STURDY ARTISAN COUNTRY BREAD

FRESHLY GROUND BLACK PEPPER

1. Wash and pick over the dried beans. Put them in a bowl with 1.25 litres cold water. Leave to stand overnight at room temperature, or up to 3 days, chilled. Alternatively, quick-soak the dried beans by putting them in a saucepan with 1.25 litres water. Bring to the boil, cover, remove from heat and leave to stand for 1 hour.

2. Transfer the rehydrated beans with their soaking water to an ample saucepan. Add 5 of the garlic cloves, the sage sprig and the 3 tablespoons olive oil. Bring to the boil and immediately reduce to a steady simmer. Cook gently over medium-low heat until the beans are tender, about 1 hour. There should be a ratio of about 1 part cooked beans to 2 parts bean stock. Add 2 teaspoons salt, cover and set aside until the salt is absorbed, about 15 minutes. Taste and adjust salt if necessary; fish out and discard the sage.

3. Toast the bread lightly; rub on both sides with the remaining garlic clove. Place two of the bread slices in each of four individual soup bowls; drizzle with olive oil. Pour a ladleful of the hot beans and some of their liquid over each piece of bread. Sprinkle generously with freshly ground black pepper and drizzle with additional olive oil to taste. Serve at once.

5

PASTA BY HEART –
PLUS GRAIN, POLENTA, RICE AND BEAN DISHES

Pasta, polenta and beans are the comfort zone and foundation stone of Italian comfort food. Pasta is a national food, but its great importance is as a symbol of triumph over hunger in the poor south. The anthropologist Professor Folco Portinari says Italians rank it 'somewhere between a sacrament and a psychotropic drug'. Polenta and beans are regional. Before pasta, cheap, plentiful and nutritious beans fed the common people. Pellegrino Artusi, author of the first national Italian cookbook, called them 'the meat of the poor'. Northern Italy's coarse-ground cornmeal, polenta, has similar stature: folklore tells of peasants who, given a rare ration of meat, stunned their benefactor by selling it to buy polenta. Of course: Meat would make a meal; polenta would feed a family. Here I include my favourite pasta, grain, polenta and beans recipes, all of which have been passed down from generation to generation through grandmothers, aunts or the ladies next door.

SAFFRON FREGULA
Makes 35oz

My great aunt Maria ('Mariedda' in dialect) lived in Iglesias, an ancient mining city on the south coast of Sardinia that was founded by the Phoenicians. She made pasta at home every day until she was 102 years old. This is her traditional method for *fregula,* the hand-formed semolina 'crumb' pasta that is unique to the island. You can make the 'crumbs' small or large; small *fregula* are added to soups and the large are combined with meat or seafood in baked dishes, or used like macaroni in *pasta e fagioli* and other dishes. They can be used fresh or dried for future use.

APPROXIMATELY 160ML COLD WATER 400G FINE SEMOLINA FLOUR

1 SACHET SAFFRON POWDER

1. Whisk together the water and the saffron.

2. Spread some of the semolina on the bottom of a large, shallow mixing bowl, preferably made of wood, and sprinkle it with enough of the water to form little 'crumbs' from the moistened semolina with your hands. As you work, keep your hands rotating in the bowl, using your fingers to combine the flour and water to form the *fregula.* As the pasta 'crumbs' are formed, keep adding semolina and sprinkling water until all of the semolina is used. If more water is necessary, pour some cold water into a small bowl. It is easier to dip your free hand in to sprinkle, rather than to measure out amounts of water to add to the flour. The 'crumbs' should be well formed but raggy looking and not too wet. If they are too wet, add a little more semolina and work it through the *fregula.* Spread the 'crumbs' out on a baking tray, cover with clean tea towels and leave to rest at room temperature for 20 to 30 minutes or up to 24 hours.

3. Add the *fregula* to a stock or soup like any other pasta. Or boil them in plenty of salted water for about 12 minutes; drain and toss with a smooth tomato sauce (see chapter 2).

4. To dry *fregula* for future use, preheat the oven to 90°C/200°F/gas mark ¼. Slide the baking tray on the middle rack and bake until thoroughly dried, about 1 hour. Shake occasionally to allow for even drying. Leave to cool, then store in an airtight container for up to 1 month.

THE AUTHENTIC
SPAGHETTI ALLA CARBONARA

Serves 4

Most versions of *spaghetti alla carbonara* outside of Italy include cream, but there is no cream in the genuine recipe, which dates from World War Two. By some accounts, Italian women invented the new sauce for pasta when presented with bacon and egg rations by their American GI lovers. In any case, the sauce ingredients and method here are considered by Italian culinary historians to be the original and authentic version. While *carbonara* sauce was designed for spaghetti, I find fusilli are also a pleasant cut to use because the sauce collects nicely in its grooves.

5 EGGS, BEATEN

75G FRESHLY GRATED GRANA PADANO
OR PARMIGIANO-REGGIANO CHEESE,
PLUS EXTRA TO SERVE

SEA SALT AND FRESHLY GROUND
BLACK PEPPER

450G IMPORTED ITALIAN SPAGHETTI
OR FUSILLI

2 TABLESPOONS KOSHER SALT

4 TABLESPOONS EXTRA-VIRGIN OLIVE OIL

225G PANCETTA OR GUANCIALE (CHEEK
BACON), THICKLY SLICED AND DICED

1. In a bowl, combine the beaten eggs with the grated cheese and season with salt and pepper.

2. Select a serving bowl for the pasta and keep it warm.

3. Fill a saucepan with 4.7 litres water and bring it to a rapid boil over high heat. Add the spaghetti or fusilli and the kosher salt together and stir. Check the packet instructions for cooking time. Cook, stirring frequently, until the pasta is 2 minutes away from being al dente.

4. Meanwhile, in a large frying pan, warm the olive oil. Add the pancetta or guanciale and sauté over medium heat until nicely coloured and crispy. Set aside.

5. When the pasta is ready, drain it, reserving about 250ml of the cooking water. Transfer it to the frying pan with the pancetta and toss over low heat. Add 125ml or so of the cooking water to moisten. Simmer until the water is nearly evaporated.

6. Remove the frying pan from the heat, transfer the pasta to the serving bowl and immediately add the egg and cheese mixture, tossing vigorously to distribute the sauce while making sure it does not coagulate into scrambled egg. It should not exceed 70°C. If the pasta seems dry, add more of the reserved cooking water. Serve at once, passing the pepper mill and the grated cheese at the table.

CAPPELLINI with TOMATO and PANCETTA

Serves 4

My aunt Rita grew up in a convent in Cagliari during the war when food was hard to come by even on the pastoral island of Sardinia. But the nuns made whatever provisions they did have taste good by using local aromatics skilfully. Whether my aunt picked up that gift for simple but artful cooking from the good sisters, or whether she inherited her instincts from her father, a legendary connoisseur of good food and wine, her flare for elevating simple ingredients is evident in this zesty, quick and easy pasta dish, which can be assembled and cooked in less than half an hour. If using bacon in place of pancetta, blanch it for 1 minute before chopping. The hot pepper adds a nice pep.

2 TABLESPOONS EXTRA-VIRGIN OLIVE OIL

225G PANCETTA OR BLANCHED BACON, CHOPPED

1 ONION, CHOPPED

2 LARGE GARLIC CLOVES, SMASHED

10 TO 20 HOT RED PEPPERS, DESEEDED AND CHOPPED

1 800-G TIN ITALIAN PLUM TOMATOES, CRUSHED

SEA SALT

450G IMPORTED ITALIAN CAPPELLINI

2 TABLESPOONS KOSHER SALT

FRESHLY GRATED PECORINO CHEESE, TO SERVE

1. In a large frying pan, warm the olive oil over medium-low heat. Add the pancetta or bacon, onion, garlic and hot peppers. Sauté until the mixture is lightly coloured and aromatic, about 10 minutes. Drain off some but not all of the excess fat, as it adds terrific flavour to the sauce. Stir in the tomatoes and salt to taste.

2. In the meantime, in a saucepan, bring 4.7 litres water to a rapid boil over high heat. Add the pasta and kosher salt all at once and stir. Consult the cooking time on the packet and cook over high heat, stirring frequently, until the pasta is 3 minutes short of done. Drain, reserving 250ml or so of the pasta water should you need it later.

3. Transfer the cappellini to the frying pan with the sauce and cook over medium heat, tossing frequently, for 2 minutes, or until the pasta is al dente. If necessary, add some of the reserved pasta water to moisten. Serve at once, passing the grated cheese at the table.

CAPPELLINI AGLIO E OLIO
Serves 4

Another of my aunt's triumphs in simple cooking. Because cappellini are very fine, they can overcook all too easily. *Fidellini,* which are slightly thicker than *cappellini,* work even better here, but they aren't as easy to find in supermarkets. This departure from the usual way of cooking them works very well. This dish is terrific on its own, or it makes a happy union with many meat or poultry dishes.

½ TEASPOON RED PEPPER FLAKES

175ML EXTRA-VIRGIN OLIVE OIL

12 LARGE GARLIC CLOVES, CHOPPED

SEA SALT

450G IMPORTED ITALIAN CAPPELLINI OR FIDELLINI

2 TABLESPOONS KOSHER SALT

45G FRESH BASIL, CUT INTO JULIENNE

1. Warm the red pepper flakes in a large frying pan over medium-low heat. Add the olive oil and warm. Add the garlic. Sauté until the garlic is an even golden colour. Turn off the heat at once.

2. When you are ready to eat, in a saucepan bring 4.7 litres water to a rapid boil over high heat. Add the pasta and kosher salt together and stir. Cover and turn off the heat. Allow to rest until the pasta is al dente. Drain, reserving 250ml or so of the pasta water should you need it later.

3. Transfer the *cappellini* to the frying pan, add the basil and toss all together. If necessary, add some of the reserved pasta cooking water to moisten. Serve at once.

SPAGHETTI with SAUTÉED RADICCHIO

Serves 2 to 4

I corresponded with Paolo Lanapoppi, a Venetian writer and gondola restorer, for some time before I finally tracked him down in Venice. When we finally met, the radicchio of nearby Treviso was in full flower, and he cooked up this delightful homespun dish for lunch over talk of *carnevale* and gondolas. Paolo topped the pasta generously with Parmigiano-Reggiano cheese at the table, but it is equally delicious without the cheese.

6 TABLESPOONS EXTRA-VIRGIN OLIVE OIL

1 RED ONION, THINLY SLICED AND THEN CHOPPED

225 TO 275G RADICCHIO, PREFERABLY THE ELONGATED TARDIVO VARIETY, CUT INTO JULIENNE AND THEN ROUGHLY CHOPPED

125ML HOT WATER

½ TEASPOON SEA SALT, OR TO TASTE

350G IMPORTED ITALIAN SPAGHETTI

2 TABLESPOONS KOSHER SALT

FRESHLY GROUND BLACK PEPPER

FRESHLY GRATED PARMIGIANO-REGGIANO CHEESE, TO SERVE

1. In an ample frying pan, warm the olive oil over medium-low heat. Add the onion and sauté until nicely softened and lightly coloured, about 6 minutes. Toss in the radicchio, and use a wooden spoon to coat it evenly in the olive oil. Add the water, continuing to toss. Cover and continue to cook over medium-low heat, stirring occasionally, until the radicchio is tender, 10 to 12 minutes. Add the sea salt, cover and set aside.

2. Bring a large saucepan filled with water over high heat to a rolling boil. Stir in the pasta and kosher salt. Cook, always over the highest heat possible and stirring constantly to prevent the pasta strands from sticking together, until the spaghetti is almost cooked, about 6 minutes. Add a glass of cold water to the pan to arrest the boiling and drain immediately, setting aside about 250ml of the cooking water. Add the spaghetti to the frying pan, and return the heat to high. Use 2 long forks to distribute all the ingredients evenly, about 1 minute. If necessary, add a little of the pasta water to moisten so that everything mixes nicely together. Serve immediately with plenty of pepper and pass the Parmigiano-Reggiano cheese at the table.

SPAGHETTI WITH CLAM SAUCE,
RED VERSION

Serves 4

Is there any dish more reminiscent than this one of the proverbial Italian repast eaten by moonlight at some romantic seaside spot – say, Amalfi or Sorrento? It was not until I took my first trip to southern Italy as a young woman that I knew what this dish should really taste like, and perhaps it was the grip of romance that made it so indescribably beguiling. But even in my American kitchen, there is a certain magic in it, and I cook it regularly. Note that grated cheese should never be added to seafood sauces for pasta.

100G SEA SALT, PLUS EXTRA FOR SEASONING

150G CORNMEAL

1.8KG COCKLES OR MANILA CLAMS, OR 4 DOZEN SMALL LITTLENECK CLAMS

75ML EXTRA-VIRGIN OLIVE OIL

6 LARGE GARLIC CLOVES, CRUSHED

4 TABLESPOONS CHOPPED FRESH FLAT-LEAF PARSLEY

3 LARGE RIPE TOMATOES, PEELED, DESEEDED, AND CHOPPED, OR 200G TINNED PLUM TOMATOES, DRAINED, DESEEDED AND CHOPPED

125ML CLAM JUICE OR GOOD-QUALITY DRY WHITE WINE

FRESHLY GROUND BLACK PEPPER

2 TABLESPOONS KOSHER SALT

450G SPAGHETTI OR THIN LINGUINE

CRUSTY ARTISAN BREAD, TO SERVE

1. Mix the salt and cornmeal in 4 litres water and soak the clams for 3 to 4 hours so that they purge themselves of sand or other matter. (Make sure you use sea or kosher salt, as the iodine in regular salt will kill the clams before they hit the boiling water.) One hour before cooking, scrub the clams well with a stiff vegetable brush under cold running water and rinse them until they are free of sand. Before cooking, tap any open clams. If they close, keep them; if not, discard at once.

2. In a large frying pan over medium-low heat, warm the olive oil. Add the garlic and parsley, and cook until the garlic is lightly coloured, about 5 minutes. Add the tomatoes and allow to simmer over medium heat for 2 to 3 minutes. Add the clam juice or wine and simmer gently for 3 to 4 minutes. Add the scrubbed clams, cover tightly and steam over medium heat until the clams open. Add sea salt and pepper to taste. Lift out any empty shells, and discard any clams that did not open. You can use the sauce with the clams in their shells or, if preferred, shell some of the clams and leave the remainder in their shells for effect. (It's fun to suck the tasty clams out of their shells, digging in with your hands, as the Italians do.)

3. While the clams are cooking, in a pot, bring 4.7 litres water to a rapid boil over high heat. Add the 2 tablespoons kosher salt and the pasta. Stir immediately and continue to stir occasionally to prevent the strands from sticking together. Cook for 1 minute less than indicated on the packet directions for al dente. Drain well and immediately add the pasta to the clam sauce in the frying pan and toss. Serve immediately and pass the bread at the table for soaking up the sauce – not a drop should go to waste!

LINGUINE WITH TUNA SAUCE AND PARSLEY

Serves 4 to 6

This sauce might be overlooked because it is made with tinned tuna, but premium Italian tuna cut from the belly of the fish is pink, tender and sweet, and it dissolves easily into a delicious and quick sauce for pasta. White albacore tuna or tuna packed in its own juices or in spring water won't do; they are just too dry for this sauce.

5 TABLESPOONS EXTRA-VIRGIN OLIVE OIL

4 LARGE GARLIC CLOVES, SMASHED

1 TEASPOON FINELY CHOPPED FRESH THYME

5 TABLESPOONS CHOPPED FRESH FLAT-LEAF PARSLEY

200-G TIN PREMIUM ITALIAN TUNA PACKED IN OLIVE OIL, DRAINED AND FINELY CHOPPED

125ML GOOD-QUALITY DRY WHITE WINE

PINCH OF RED PEPPER FLAKES

450G IMPORTED ITALIAN THIN LINGUINE

2 TABLESPOONS KOSHER SALT

1. In a large frying pan, warm the oil. Add the garlic and sauté over medium-low heat until it is soft and fragrant, about 2 minutes. Stir in the thyme, half the parsley and the tuna. Add the wine to the pan to form a sauce. Add the pepper flakes and simmer for 5 minutes over medium-low heat. Add the remaining parsley.

2. Bring 4.7 litres water in a saucepan to a rapid boil over high heat. Add the pasta and the kosher salt to the boiling water and cook according to packet instructions over high heat, stirring. When it is cooked 1 minute less than al dente, drain, reserving 125ml of the cooking water.

3. Transfer the pasta to the frying pan with the tuna sauce and toss all together. If necessary, add a few tablespoons of the pasta water to add moisture. Serve at once.

NONNA DOMENICA'S
MACARONI WITH BROCCOLI SAUCE

Serves 4

This rustic dish is a speciality of Puglia, a part of southern Italy from which many immigrants came – my own paternal grandparents included. It never ceases to evoke in me a renewed awe for real, exuberant southern Italian food of the sort most Americans rarely experience. My sisters and I loved this pasta so much that we fought for it if any was left at the bottom of the bowl – even after we had had second helpings. My mother eventually learned to make double what she usually made, and the next day for lunch, she warmed up the leftovers in a frying pan until it was hot and crisp – and we fought over that, too! Don't be put off by the anchovies in the sauce; they dissolve completely into the hot olive oil to form the sauce. Even avowed anchovy haters for whom I have made this dish have loved it. Note: don't add grated cheese, please.

1 LARGE HEAD BROCCOLI

2 TABLESPOONS KOSHER SALT

450G RIGATONI, ZITI, PENNE
OR PENNE RIGATE

125ML EXTRA-VIRGIN OLIVE OIL

1½ TINS ANCHOVY FILLETS PRESERVED
IN OLIVE OIL

1. Wash and trim the broccoli, cutting off any tough or discoloured parts. Divide the top part into florets and slice the stalks into 5-cm pieces.

2. In an ample saucepan, bring 6.6 litres water to a rapid boil. Stir in the salt, the broccoli, and the pasta all at once. Cook over high heat until the pasta is al dente and the broccoli is soft and creamy. Stir several times as the pasta cooks to prevent it from sticking together and to allow even cooking.

3. Meanwhile, in a large frying pan, warm the olive oil and the anchovies together, including the oil from one of the anchovy tins. The anchovies will dissolve completely in the oil, forming the basis of the sauce. Keep warm.

4. When the pasta is cooked, drain it, but don't over-drain; it should still be moist and dripping a little. Toss the pasta and broccoli with the anchovy sauce in the frying pan. Serve immediately.

PUGLIA-STYLE SHORT PASTA
WITH COOL SUMMER SAUCE

Serves 4 to 6

Another dish from my father's native region that I learned from my Italian friend Anna Maria Erenbourg Weld. Anna Maria often spends her summers at her brother's home in Otranto, an ancient port on the tip of Puglia's western coastline. The best gifts she brings back are robust recipes, like this one, which she learned from a local woman who grows vegetables in her courtyard and likes to share cooking advice with her neighbours.

EXTRA-VIRGIN OLIVE OIL FOR GREASING, PLUS 125ML FOR THE SAUCE

SEA SALT

½ TEASPOON DRIED OREGANO

620G SWEET VINE-RIPENED CHERRY TOMATOES, HALVED

110G IMPORTED SMOKED OR UNSMOKED RICOTTA SALATA, OR SUBSTITUTE FETA, CRUMBLED

2 TABLESPOONS CHOPPED FRESH MINT

1 SMALL DRIED HOT RED PEPPER, DESEEDED AND FINELY CHOPPED, OR SUBSTITUTE ½ TEASPOON RED PEPPER FLAKES

450G IMPORTED ITALIAN SHORT PASTA SUCH AS PENNE OR MEDIUM-SIZE RIGATONI

2 TABLESPOONS KOSHER SALT

1. Preheat the oven to 220°C/425°F/gas mark 7.

2. Grease a baking tray with olive oil. Sprinkle lightly with sea salt and scatter the oregano. Place the cherry tomatoes, cut side down, on the tray. Slide the pan on the middle rack of the oven and bake until a liquid forms on the bottom of the tray, but no more than 10 minutes; the tomatoes should not actually cook. Reserve the tomato juices.

3. In a serving bowl, combine the 125ml olive oil, baked tomatoes, cheese, mint, red pepper and sea salt to taste.

4. In the meantime, bring 4.7 litres water in a saucepan to a rapid boil over high heat. Add the pasta and kosher salt at the same time and stir. Consult the cooking directions on the back of the pasta packet and continue to cook over high heat, stirring frequently, until the pasta is cooked al dente. Drain, transfer the pasta to the serving bowl and toss with the sauce and the reserved tomato juices. Serve at once.

STEWED LENTILS
WITH SAGE

Serves 3 to 4

Here is a popular dish that is eaten both as a meatless side dish and as a main course with roasted pork sausages. Boiling the lentils before cooking them in the sauce sweetens them naturally. For centuries, lentils have been a food of the poor, who couldn't afford the luxury of buying meat. As a result, Italian housewives have made lentil cookery into an art, such as this rib-sticking and nutritious dish infused with the flavours of a rich vegetable *battuto*, garlic and sage.

300G DRIED BROWN LENTILS

1 BAY LEAF

3 TEASPOONS SEA SALT, PLUS MORE TO TASTE

125ML EXTRA-VIRGIN OLIVE OIL, PLUS EXTRA FOR DRIZZLING

2 CARROTS, FINELY CHOPPED

1 TENDER CELERY HEART WITH LEAVES, FINELY CHOPPED

1 LARGE ONION, FINELY CHOPPED

6 LARGE GARLIC CLOVES, SMASHED

1 20CM SAGE SPRIG

500ML 20-MINUTE TOMATO SAUCE (PAGE 37) OR PASSATA

1. Rinse and pick over the lentils; drain. Put the lentils and bay leaf in a saucepan and add cold water to cover by 7.5cm. Bring to the boil. Reduce the heat to a simmer and cook until not quite tender, about 20 minutes. Skim off any foam that forms at the top. Turn off the heat, stir in the salt and leave to stand for 5 to 10 minutes. Drain and set aside, reserving the cooking liquid. Discard the bay leaf.

2. In a large frying pan, warm the 125ml olive oil and add the carrots, celery, onion, garlic and sage. Sauté, stirring occasionally, until softened, about 10 minutes. Stir in the drained lentils. Add salt to taste and the passata and enough lentil cooking liquid to cover, about 125ml, or as needed. Cover, reduce the heat to low, and simmer, stirring occasionally, until the lentils are tender, about 10 minutes. Add more lentil water as necessary to keep the lentils from drying out; the consistency of the stew should be loose but not watery.

3. Turn off the heat and leave to stand for about 10 minutes. Taste for salt, fish out the sage and serve. Drizzle a little extra-virgin olive oil over each serving for added flavour.

SIMMERED WHITE BEANS
WITH SAUSAGE AND TOMATO

A side dish for 4

When I was growing up, my mother often reminisced about the things she missed from her native Italy. The flavour of Italian beans was one of them. I have friends who carry beans back from Tuscany – the home of true bean lovers – when they go there because Tuscan beans are so flavourful. In this dish, the sauce and succulent fennel sausages give great flavour to the beans, which become saturated with their juices.

2 TABLESPOONS EXTRA-VIRGIN OLIVE OIL

1 ONION, FINELY CHOPPED

2 GARLIC CLOVES, FINELY CHOPPED

3 SWEET ITALIAN FENNEL SAUSAGES
(ABOUT 225G TOTAL WEIGHT), CASINGS
REMOVED

1 TABLESPOON TOMATO PURÉE

3 CHOPPED FRESH SAGE LEAVES OR
½ TEASPOON DRIED SAGE

125ML TASTY MEAT STOCK (PAGE 213),
OR WATER

½ TEASPOON SALT, OR TO TASTE

FRESHLY GROUND BLACK PEPPER

90G COOKED, DRAINED CANNELLINI
BEANS (PAGE 84)

1 TABLESPOON CHOPPED FRESH FLAT-
LEAF PARSLEY

1. In a frying pan over medium-low heat, warm the olive oil. Add the onion and garlic and sauté gently until totally softened but not browned, about 5 minutes. Using a slotted spoon, remove the onion and garlic from the pan and transfer to a bowl.

2. Heat the oil that remains in the pan and add the sausage meat to it, breaking it up with a wooden spoon. Sauté until browned, stirring occasionally, about 5 minutes. Return the onion and garlic to the pan. Add the tomato purée, sage, stock or water, salt and pepper to taste and bring to the boil. Add the beans, bring to the boil again and immediately reduce to a simmer. Partially cover and cook gently for 10 to 15 minutes. Sprinkle with the parsley and serve hot or warm.

NONNA GIULIA'S
POLENTA LAYER CAKE WITH MEAT SAUCE
Serves 8

My maternal grandmother's polenta cake is much like baked lasagne except that polenta replaces pasta in between layers of winey meat sauce and tangy young sheep's-milk cheese. Nonna Giulia died long before I was born, but her recipe for this provincial Sardinian dish, called *pasticciata di polenta* in Italian, was one of her jewels, and passed down by my mother.

FOR THE SAUCE

6 TABLESPOONS EXTRA-VIRGIN OLIVE OIL

1 ONION, FINELY CHOPPED

1 CARROT, CHOPPED

1 SMALL CELERY STICK WITH LEAVES, CHOPPED

1 TEASPOON GROUND FENNEL SEEDS

450G MINCED LEAN PORK, OR MIXED MINCED PORK AND BEEF

125ML GOOD-QUALITY DRY RED WINE

3 TABLESPOONS TOMATO PURÉE

1 975-G TIN PLUM TOMATOES, DRAINED, DESEEDED AND CHOPPED, JUICES RESERVED

3 TABLESPOONS FINELY CHOPPED BASIL LEAVES

1 TEASPOON SEA SALT

1 RECIPE BASIC POLENTA, PAGE 217

225G SEMISOFT PECORINO CHEESE SUCH AS FIOR DI SARDEGNA OR TUSCAN CACIOTTA, OR SUBSTITUTE SPANISH MANCHEGO, SHREDDED

OLIVE OR VEGETABLE OIL, FOR OILING POLENTA BOARD OR WORK SURFACE

1. To make the sauce, warm the oil in a frying pan. Stir in the onion, carrot and celery and continue to sauté until soft, 10 minutes. Add the fennel seeds and pork and sauté over low heat until the meat colours lightly, stirring occasionally, about 4 minutes. Stir in the wine and allow to evaporate, 1 minute. Add the tomato purée diluted in some of the reserved tomato juices followed by the tomatoes, another 125ml tomato juices, basil and the salt. Stir well. Partially cover and simmer over the lowest heat for 1 hour, stirring frequently, until the sauce is thick and fragrant. Add more tomato juices during cooking if the sauce seems to be drying out.

2. Lightly oil a 23 x 33-cm baking dish and set aside. Make the polenta and turn it out onto a lightly oiled board or work surface. Use a rubber spatula or knife dipped into hot water to spread it out into a rectangle about 5mm thick. Let stand until cooled completely and firm, about 15 minutes. Cut into 7.5-cm squares; set aside.

3. Heat an oven to 230°C/450°F/gas mark 8. Arrange half the polenta squares in the base of the baking dish. Pour half the sauce over the polenta squares and spread to cover. Sprinkle half the cheese over the sauce. Repeat with another layer of each. Bake until the 'cake' is heated through and the cheese is golden brown, between 15 and 20 minutes. Leave to stand for 10 minutes. Cut into portions and serve.

STEAMING POLENTA
WITH TALEGGIO CHEESE

Serves 4

I was first served this homey dish in Lombardy, land of sublime taleggio cheese. Taleggio and polenta is a logical marriage in this polenta-eating, cheese-producing part of Italy, and now it is standard fare in my kitchen as well. There is nothing to it: Pour steaming polenta directly from the cooking pan onto a large platter and top with hunks of this rich, buttery cheese. A few pointers: Be sure to add the polenta to the water in a slow, steady trickle, stirring all the time, to prevent lumps from forming. While I prefer unprocessed, long-cooking polenta for its creaminess and superior flavour, it can be hard to find. Substitute a Spanish brand of polenta cornmeal or organic polenta meal rather than instant polenta, which is far more pricey and not as good. Polenta should be made in time to serve it immediately, from pan to table.

4 TABLESPOONS UNSALTED BUTTER, MELTED

700G IMPORTED ITALIAN TALEGGIO CHEESE, AT ROOM TEMPERATURE

2 LITRES WATER

2 TABLESPOONS COARSE SALT

450G COARSE POLENTA CORNMEAL

ADDITIONAL BOILING WATER, IF NECESSARY

1. Drizzle the melted butter in a wide, shallow serving dish. Cut the crust off the taleggio and have it ready to spoon over the polenta after it is cooked.

2. Fill a deep, heavy saucepan with the 2 litres water and bring it to a rolling boil over high heat. Add the salt, and little by little, pour in the cornmeal, using a sturdy wooden spoon or whisk to stir well and continuously. Cook over medium heat, stirring the polenta often; this is important if the polenta is to become properly soft and creamy. The polenta is ready when it is so thick that it begins to resist stirring and pulls away easily from the sides of the pan with the spoon or whisk (40 to 50 minutes or more for unprocessed polenta; about 20 minutes for Spanish or organic polenta). If the polenta is quite thick but still not pulling away easily from the pan, add a little more boiling water and continue to stir until it is ready.

3. Pour the polenta, piping hot, into the serving dish. Spoon the taleggio, which by now has softened, on top of the polenta. Use a large serving spoon to dish the polenta and cheese onto individual plates and serve at once.

BREAD PASTICCIO

Serves 4 to 6

In Italy, this is called *lasagne povera,* or 'poor lasagne', because leftover bread is used in place of pasta. Make it in the summer when you can get fresh, sweet vine-ripened tomatoes in season. It makes a scrumptious snack or a memorable side dish.

EXTRA-VIRGIN OLIVE OIL, FOR GREASING

350G STALE BREAD, STILL SOFT ENOUGH TO CUT, CRUSTS REMOVED, THINLY SLICED

950ML TASTY MEAT STOCK (PAGE 213) OR VEGETABLE STOCK (PAGE 215)

700G SWEET, JUICY VINE-RIPENED TOMATOES, PEELED AND ROUGHLY CHOPPED

10 FRESH BASIL LEAVES, FINELY CHOPPED

2 TEASPOONS FINELY CHOPPED FRESH MARJORAM OR THYME, OR 1 TEASPOON DRIED

225G MOZZARELLA, GRATED

25G FRESHLY GRATED PARMIGIANO-REGGIANO OR GRANA PADANO

4 LARGE EGGS

60ML MILK

½ TEASPOON SALT

1. Preheat the oven to 160°C/325°F/gas mark 3. Select a 23 x 33-cm or equivalent baking dish (preferably non-stick) with high sides, and brush it generously with extra-virgin olive oil.

2. Soak half the bread in the stock until it has absorbed as much liquid as it can without falling apart. Arrange the slices on the base of the prepared baking dish. Over that, arrange a layer of the tomatoes, then scatter half of the basil and thyme. Follow with a layer of mozzarella, followed by a scattering of half the grated cheese. Soak the remaining bread and repeat the layers with the remaining ingredients.

3. Beat the eggs with the milk and the salt and pour over. Poke holes through the top to enable the egg to penetrate the lower layer. Grease well the shiny side of a piece of foil large enough to cover the dish; cover tightly. Slide the baking dish onto the centre rack of the oven and cook for 1 hour. Remove the foil and bake for another 10 minutes to allow the top to colour nicely.

4. Remove the baking dish from the oven and allow to settle for 10 to 20 minutes. Use a metal fish slice to dislodge the 'lasagne' from the sides of the dish. Cut into individual portions and serve hot or warm.

6

MAIN DISHES:
POULTRY

When I was young my Italian relatives always talked about how chickens used to taste. No wonder. The birds then roamed freely around the farm, pecking and scratching for food as the Lord intended, and were slaughtered only hours before cooking. Modern, mass-produced chickens – what my mother used to call 'factory-made' – have ruled the roost in the U.K. for decades and will continue to do so, but organic, free-range or naturally raised poultry is becoming readily available, even in supermarkets. Italians prefer their chicken on the bone (where the flavour is best), as in *pollo alla cacciatore,* and turkey, once uncommon, has become more popular. Both birds are bred small and tender in Italy, unlike the larger and less tender ones. Note that breast meat is comparatively bland and dries out easily. The dark meat is moister and more flavourful and, for the most part, the one that I include in these recipes.

ZIA ANNA'S
ROASTED CHICKEN WITH SAFFRON STUFFING
Serves 4

This beguiling recipe with its Sardinian flavours and hint of saffron transforms ordinary roast chicken into a feast. The golden-tinted, aromatic stuffing can be used for all types of fowl, including guinea fowl or turkey. If you have the giblets, liver and wattles of the bird, include them in the stuffing for added flavour. Use plain artisanal bread with no added flavourings.

2KG FREE-RANGE CHICKEN AT ROOM TEMPERATURE, INCLUDING LIVER AND GIBLETS, IF AVAILABLE

SEA SALT AND FRESHLY GROUND BLACK PEPPER

1 LARGE ONION, QUARTERED

3 TABLESPOONS EXTRA-VIRGIN OLIVE OIL, PLUS MORE FOR RUBBING INTO BIRD

2 TABLESPOONS UNSALTED BUTTER, PLUS MORE FOR FINISHING STUFFING

1 ONION, CHOPPED

2 MEDIUM CELERY STICKS, INCLUDING LEAVES, CHOPPED

3 SWEET ITALIAN PORK SAUSAGES FLAVOURED WITH FENNEL, CASINGS REMOVED

5 TABLESPOONS FRESH CHOPPED FLAT-LEAF PARSLEY

5 FRESH BASIL LEAVES, CHOPPED

8 SUN-DRIED TOMATO HALVES, RECONSTITUTED AND CHOPPED

300G DICED PACKED, DAY-OLD BREAD, CRUSTS REMOVED

¼ TEASPOON SAFFRON THREADS, OR 2 SACHETS PURE SAFFRON POWDER

360ML CHICKEN STOCK (PAGE 214), OR MORE IF NEEDED

1. Preheat an oven to 230°C/450°F/gas mark 8. Wash the chicken in cold water and dry thoroughly, inside and out. Sprinkle the cavity with salt and pepper and stuff with the quartered onion; fasten closed with cocktail sticks and truss the bird, keeping the wings and legs close to the body. If using giblets, wash and dry them. Discard the whitish membrane on the gizzard and chop coarse. Set the bird aside at room temperature.

2. In an ample frying pan, warm the olive oil and butter over medium heat and add the onion and celery. Sauté for about 8 minutes, stirring occasionally. Add the giblets and sausage and sauté gently, stirring occasionally, until browned and cooked through, another 8 minutes. Add the parsley, basil and sun-dried tomatoes. Sauté until soft. Stir in the bread and sauté for another few minutes to coat it.

3. Dissolve the saffron powder in 240ml of the stock. Pour it over the bread in the frying pan and combine thoroughly. Season with salt and pepper. Taste to ensure that the stuffing is moist. If it is too dry, add up to another 120ml stock. Transfer to a buttered medium baking dish. Dot the surface with butter, cover with buttered foil and refrigerate until ready to bake.

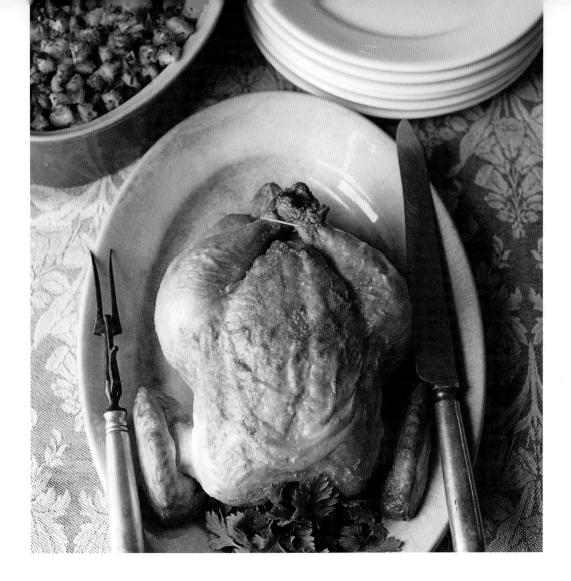

4. Place the chicken on a rack in a roasting tin just the right size. Rub the skin lightly with olive oil. Sprinkle 2 teaspoons salt on the surface of the bird for a nice uniform coating and crisp, flavourful skin. Place the bird breast side down. Pour 5mm stock in the base of the roasting tin.

5. Reduce the oven temperature to 190°C/375°F/gas mark 5 and set the chicken on the middle rack. Roast the chicken for 30 minutes. Remove and breast side up. Roast for another 30 minutes. Turn breast-side down for the last stretch. Baste each time you take the chicken out of the oven to turn it. In total, roast the bird for 20 minutes per 450g, or until a thermometer slipped into the thigh registers 71 .1°C, or the juices run clear when pierced. About 15 minutes before the chicken is finished, slide the stuffing on the rack next to the bird and cook for 20 to 25 minutes, removing the foil during the last 5 minutes to form a golden crust.

6. Remove the chicken from the oven, tent with foil and allow to settle for 15 minutes. De-fat the juices from the tin to pass at the table. Remove the string on the bird, carve and sprinkle with pepper. Serve, spooning some stuffing onto each dish.

WHOLE ROASTED CHICKEN
WITH GARLIC, FRESH GARDEN HERBS AND GRAVY

Serves 4

My first lesson in procuring chicken took place as a girl on a trip to the Cagliari market with my aunt Anna. She went from stall to stall, asking the meat purveyors if their chicken was 'machine-made' or not. If it wasn't raised in a barnyard, pecking and scratching for grubs and grasses, she wouldn't have any part of it. Here was one of her methods for roasting those succulent free-range chickens, which is easily done in a home oven or outdoors on a spit.

2KG FREE-RANGE ROASTING CHICKEN, AT ROOM TEMPERATURE

2 TEASPOONS FENNEL SEEDS, GROUND

HANDFUL OF FRESH THYME, TWIGS AND LEAVES

LARGE PINCH OF CAYENNE PEPPER

12 GARLIC CLOVES, SMASHED

SEA SALT

HANDFUL OF FRESH SAGE, TWIGS AND LEAVES

HANDFUL OF FRESH ROSEMARY, TWIGS AND LEAVES

500ML CHICKEN STOCK (PAGE 214)

75ML GOOD-QUALITY DRY WHITE WINE

1. Preheat the oven to 220°C/425°F/gas mark 7. Remove excess fat from the chicken. Wash it inside and out under cold running water and use strong kitchen paper to pat it thoroughly dry.

2. In a small bowl, mix the fennel, thyme and cayenne pepper. Rub the inside of the cavity with one garlic clove and half the spice mixture. Sprinkle with salt. Place all the garlic and most of the herbs inside, reserving some for garnish. Rub the outside of the bird with the remaining spice mixture, loosely tie the legs together, and place breast side up in a roasting tin. Pour the stock to reach 5mm up the sides.

3. Roast for 30 minutes. Reduce the heat to 200°C/400°F/gas mark 6, then turn the bird breast-side down for another 30 minutes. Baste every 15 minutes with tin juices, adding more stock as it evaporates. Turn breast-side up and roast for another 20 minutes, or until an instant-read thermometer reads 71.1°C. Transfer to a carving board and cover loosely with foil. Leave it to rest before carving.

4. To make the gravy, pour the tin juices through a fine mesh strainer. Transfer it to a fat separator and set aside. Warm the roasting tin over over medium heat. Add the wine and use a wooden spoon to dislodge any bits stuck to the bottom of the tin. Simmer for 2 minutes. Strain the liquid into the fat separator as well.

5. Carve the bird and arrange nicely on a warm platter. Discard the herbs from the cavity. Add juices that have collected during carving to the gravy you have made. Garnish with the reserved fresh herbs and serve at once.

ANNA AMENDOLARA'S
BAKED CHICKEN WITH TOMATOES AND GARLIC

Serves 4

Anna Amendolara Nurse is a beloved mentor to culinary stars and students alike – or anyone else who comes her way and wants to learn about Italian cooking. I especially love her homey southern Italian dishes because they hark back to the food of my own paternal ancestors, who came from the same town in Puglia as Anna's parents. This exceptional yet easy dish cries for fresh summer vine-ripened tomatoes, but imported tinned Italian plum tomatoes can be substituted successfully. This dish creates profuse tin juices, so plan on having plenty of good artisan bread on hand, or toss the juices with 225g of freshly cooked pasta. Alternatively, serve the chicken as a main course with salad and reserve the extra tin juices for fortifying another sauce or a soup.

1.6KG WHOLE FREE-RANGE CHICKEN

8 FRESH VINE-RIPENED PLUM TOMATOES, OR 8 DRAINED IMPORTED TINNED ITALIAN PLUM TOMATOES

3 LARGE GARLIC CLOVES, SLICED

3 TABLESPOONS COARSELY CHOPPED FRESH FLAT-LEAF PARSLEY

75ML EXTRA-VIRGIN OLIVE OIL

SEA SALT AND FRESHLY GROUND BLACK PEPPER

1. Preheat the oven to 200°C/400°F/gas mark 6. Wash and dry the chicken. Cut through the breast to open the chicken like a book.

2. Cut off the stem end of the tomatoes. With your hands, break open each tomato and squeeze out excess seeds and juice. Scatter half the tomatoes on the base of a roasting tin large enough to accommodate the chicken. Lay the chicken, skin-side down, over the tomatoes. Scatter the remaining tomatoes, the garlic and parsley on top of the chicken, drizzle with olive oil and season with salt and pepper. Add 125ml water to the tin.

3. Bake until the chicken is lightly browned on top, about 30 minutes. Turn the chicken over, rearranging the tomatoes and garlic on top. Bake until the chicken skin is nicely browned, about 30 to 40 minutes, or until an instant-read meat thermometer inserted into the thickest part of the thigh away from the bone registers 74°C. Add a little more water if the tin juices seem to be drying up; no more than a tablespoon or two, if any, should be necessary. Baste the chicken occasionally as it bakes to keep the breast meat moist. Remove the chicken from the oven and allow to settle for 15 minutes before carving. Serve hot.

CHICKEN CUTLETS WITH CRUNCHY COATING
AND ROCKET AND TOMATO TOPPING

Serves 4

Italians prefer chicken on the bone to comparatively bland-tasting breast meat, but creating a crunchy bread coating and adding a topping of rocket and sweet tomatoes transforms dry cutlets into a succulent dish. Turkey breast cutlets or veal cutlets can be used interchangeably with chicken breasts for this easy but elegant dish.

FOR THE SAUCE

60ML EXTRA-VIRGIN OLIVE OIL

¼ TEASPOON SALT, OR TO TASTE

FRESHLY GROUND BLACK PEPPER

450G FRESH, SWEET, MATURE VINE-RIPENED TOMATOES

1 SMALL BUNCH ROCKET (TO YIELD 25G PACKED LEAVES)

2 TABLESPOONS FINELY CHOPPED VIDALIA OR RED ONION

2 WHOLE CHICKEN BREASTS, DE-BONED AND PARTIALLY FROZEN

2 LARGE EGGS, BEATEN

1 TABLESPOON GRATED ONION

SEA SALT AND FRESHLY GROUND BLACK PEPPER

130G LIGHTLY TOASTED PANKO CRUMBS OR WHITE BREADCRUMBS

6 TABLESPOONS EXTRA-VIRGIN OLIVE OIL, OR AS NEEDED

1. To make the sauce, combine the olive oil, salt and pepper to taste in a serving bowl. Cut out each tomato core and cut the tomatoes in half lengthways. Push out the excess seeds, chop the tomatoes coarse and add to the bowl.

2. Wash the rocket under cold running water then drain. Remove the stems and yellow leaves and dry thoroughly. Chop coarse and add it and the onion to the sauce. Toss well and leave at room temperature for 30 minutes to 2 hours.

3. Put the chicken breasts on a cutting board and separate them where they naturally divide down the middle. Using a very sharp knife, slice each breast section laterally into 3 slices to make very thin, even cutlets. Beat together the eggs, grated onion, salt and pepper. Spread the panko or breadcrumbs on a piece of greaseproof paper.

4. Heat the oil in a sauté pan until it is hot enough for the chicken to sizzle. Just before frying, dip each cutlet into the egg mixture to coat on both sides, then into the crumbs, patting each to cover completely. Sauté the breasts over medium heat until they are golden on the outside but still tender and moist within, 2 to 3 minutes on each side. Drain on kitchen paper. Bread the second batch of cutlets just before slipping them into the pan. Repeat the frying and draining procedure.

5. Transfer to serving plates and spoon sauce on top. Pass more sauce at the table.

PEPPERY FRIED CHICKEN WINGS
WITH GARLIC AND ROSEMARY

Serves 4

This is one of my favourite ways of making chicken wings, adapted from a recipe for fried chicken that I learned to make from a Tuscan woman I knew. The chicken becomes crispy outside and aromatic and succulent inside, with a terrific little kick from the cayenne pepper. If you like it hot, add more cayenne pepper.

16 CHICKEN WINGS, AT ROOM TEMPERATURE

8 LARGE GARLIC CLOVES, FINELY CHOPPED

4 TABLESPOONS FINELY CHOPPED FRESH ROSEMARY, OR 2 TABLESPOONS CRUSHED DRIED ROSEMARY

185G UNBLEACHED PLAIN FLOUR

SEA SALT

¼ TEASPOON CAYENNE PEPPER

3 LARGE EGGS

GRAPESEED, SAFFLOWER OR OTHER VEGETABLE OIL, FOR FRYING

1. Wash the wings and pat dry thoroughly with kitchen paper. Keep the wing tips intact and cut the wings at the joint to separate the drummettes. In a bowl, combine the wings with the garlic and rosemary, and massage the herbs into the meat.

2. Spread the flour on a sheet of greaseproof paper. Season with salt and plenty of cayenne pepper. Beat the eggs in a wide bowl next to the greaseproof paper. Place a large platter, lined with a double layer of kitchen paper, and additional kitchen paper, nearby.

3. Pour the oil to a depth of about 2.5cm in a large, heavy-bottomed frying pan and warm over medium heat until sizzling hot. Just before you are ready to begin frying, lightly dredge each piece of wing in the flour. Dip the wing piece into the beaten eggs to coat, then dredge lightly in the flour once again. (Keep in mind that if the chicken is coated in flour and egg and left to sit for even a few minutes, the coating will become soggy and the chicken will not be crisp and light.)

4. Slip the chicken wing pieces into the hot oil, piece by piece. Do not crowd the pan with too many pieces at once, or they will not cook evenly. Fry until golden and thoroughly cooked through to the bone, about 10 minutes in total for each piece, depending on the size. Transfer to the kitchen paper. Turn each wing piece over on the paper in order to ensure that excess oil is absorbed from both sides, using additional kitchen paper as necessary to drain thoroughly.

5. When all of the chicken is cooked and drained, remove the kitchen paper from the platter, sprinkle the chicken with salt, and serve immediately.

TART CHICKEN ALLA CACCIATORA
Serves 4

Alla cacciatora, meaning 'cooked the hunter's way', probably once described methods for cooking game, but Italians use the term today to mean any number of stovetop methods for cooking every kind of meat, domesticated or otherwise. No doubt it was the hunter's wife who did the cooking. Such is the case at Ristorante Cibocchi, a little out-of-the-way *trattoria* in the region of Umbria where the owner's aunt is behind the stove. Her version of chicken *alla cacciatora* is a zesty combination of chopped lemon, peel and all, fresh rosemary, and sage.

1.6KG FREE-RANGE OR ORGANIC CHICKEN, INCLUDING GIBLETS, CUT UP

6 TABLESPOONS EXTRA-VIRGIN OLIVE OIL

5 GARLIC CLOVES, CUT INTO SMALL PIECES

½ ONION, CHOPPED

2 TEASPOONS FINELY CHOPPED FRESH ROSEMARY, OR 1 TEASPOON CRUMBLED DRIED ROSEMARY

1 TEASPOON FINELY CHOPPED FRESH SAGE, OR ½ TEASPOON DRIED SAGE

60G PITTED, BRINE-CURED TART GREEN OLIVES SUCH AS PICHOLINE, SLICED

125ML PLUS 2 TABLESPOONS GOOD-QUALITY DRY WHITE WINE

1½ TABLESPOONS WHITE WINE VINEGAR

1 TABLESPOON CAPERS, DRAINED AND FINELY CHOPPED

1 LEMON SLICE, 5MM THICK, DESEEDED AND FINELY CHOPPED, INCLUDING PEEL

PINCH OF RED PEPPER FLAKES

½ TEASPOON SEA SALT, OR TO TASTE

1. Rinse the chicken pieces, dry well and trim off all excess fat. Trim any dark spots, fat and membrane from the liver and heart and dice. Trim the tough outer layer from the gizzards and chop.

2. In a deep, heavy-bottomed frying pan big enough for all of the chicken pieces without crowding, warm the olive oil over medium-high heat. When it is sizzling hot, add the chicken pieces. Allow them to brown nicely and evenly on all sides, about 15 minutes. Transfer the chicken to a plate and set aside.

3. Drain off a tablespoon or two of the fat from the pan. Add the garlic, onion, rosemary and sage, all at once. Sauté over low heat until the garlic and onion are thoroughly cooked but not browned, 5 to 7 minutes. Return the chicken to the frying pan, and olives. Use a wooden spoon to toss the ingredients together. Pour in the wine and add the vinegar, capers, lemon, red pepper flakes and salt. Cover partially and cook until the chicken is done or registers 74°C on an instant-read thermometer, about 20 minutes. Add up to 125ml water if the chicken dries out.

4. Transfer the chicken and its sauce to a warmed platter and serve immediately.

LUISA PETRUCCI'S
OVEN-FRIED CHICKEN WITH BREADCRUMBS

Serves 4

I heard about Luisa Petrucci's home cooking from her daughter, who talked so lovingly about her mother's food that I couldn't resist asking for her recipes. Luisa emigrated from Umbria, but learned to cook from her Sicilian mother-in-law. This Sicilian version of oven-fried chicken with its delightfully crunchy coating and moist, tender meat is so similar to deep-fried chicken that you'll hardly be able to tell the difference.

EXTRA-VIRGIN OLIVE OIL

1.6KG CUT-UP FREE-RANGE OR ORGANIC CHICKEN AND ITS LIVER

90G LIGHTLY TOASTED PANKO CRUMBS OR BREADCRUMBS

25G FINELY, FRESHLY GRATED PARMIGIANO-REGGIANO, PECORINO ROMANO, OR GRANA PADANO CHEESE

3 LARGE GARLIC CLOVES, FINELY CHOPPED

3 TABLESPOONS FINELY CHOPPED FRESH FLAT-LEAF PARSLEY

1 TEASPOON SEA SALT

FRESHLY GROUND BLACK PEPPER

3 LARGE EGGS, BEATEN

1 TEASPOON MILK

1. Preheat the oven to 180°C/350°F/gas mark 4. Grease an ample roasting tin with olive oil.

2. Trim excess fat from the chicken pieces and discard. Trim any fat or membranes from the liver. Wash the chicken and pat dry with absorbent kitchen paper. Keep the wing tips intact and cut the wings at the joint to separate the drummettes.

3. Combine the breadcrumbs, grated cheese, garlic, parsley, salt and pepper to taste and spread on a sheet of greaseproof paper or on a platter. Beat the eggs and milk in a wide bowl next to the greaseproof paper. Roll the chicken pieces in the crumb mixture. Dip each piece in the beaten egg and roll once again in the crumb mixture. Arrange them in the roasting tin. Drizzle evenly with olive oil.

4. Bake the chicken until golden and cooked through, about 30 minutes for breast pieces and 40 minutes for dark meat, or until an instant-read meat thermometer registers 71.1°C. Be careful not to overcook. Allow the chicken to settle for 10 minutes before serving hot.

DONATELLA PLATONI'S
ANGRY CHICKEN

Serves 4

My friend Donatella Platoni comes from farming stock, so when she invited me to her country house near Perugia to eat *pollo all'arrabbiata,* a signature local dish, I wasn't surprised to hear her reprimanding her butcher about some chickens he had just delivered. She had placed an order for the slaughtered birds to include the stomachs as proof that they had been fed grain. The stomachs of these birds showed no trace of grain, so she sent them back and a fresh batch with grain-filled stomachs was delivered to the house within the hour.

2 YOUNG FREE-RANGE OR ORGANIC POUSSINS WITH GIBLETS, 700–900G POUNDS EACH, CUT INTO SERVING PIECES, OR 1 LARGER FREE-RANGE OR ORGANIC CHICKEN WITH GIBLETS, ABOUT 1.6KG, CUT INTO SERVING PIECES

5 TABLESPOONS EXTRA-VIRGIN OLIVE OIL

½ SMALL ONION, CUT INTO WEDGES WITH CORE ATTACHED

6 LARGE GARLIC CLOVES, CRUSHED

1 SMALL DRIED RED CHILLI, OR ¼ TEASPOON OR MORE RED PEPPER FLAKES

1 TEASPOON FINELY CHOPPED FRESH ROSEMARY OR ½ TEASPOON CRUMBLED DRIED ROSEMARY

125ML DRY WHITE WINE

200G PEELED, DESEEDED AND CHOPPED PLUM TOMATOES, DRAINED

½ TEASPOON SEA SALT, OR TO TASTE

1. Rinse the chicken pieces and dry well. Trim any dark spots, fat and membrane from the liver(s) and heart(s) and cut into quarters. Trim the tough outer layer from the gizzard(s), then chop. Set all aside.

2. In a cold, deep, heavy-bottomed non-stick frying pan, big enough to fit the chicken without crowding (or sauté in two batches), warm the olive oil. Add the chicken and giblets, raise the heat to medium, and sauté until browned nicely on all sides, about 20 minutes. Transfer to a plate and set aside.

3. Add the onion, garlic, whole chilli or red pepper flakes and rosemary and sauté gently until the garlic and onion are softened but not browned, about 8 minutes.

4. Return the chicken to the pan and pour in the wine. Stir all the ingredients together, taking care not to tear the chicken pieces. Use a metal fish slice to gently detach any piece that may stick to the bottom of the pan, so as to leave all the pieces intact. When the alcohol has evaporated, after about 3 minutes, distribute the tomatoes evenly in the pan. Reduce the heat to medium-low and cook until the chicken is tender and registers 74°C on an instant-read meat thermometer, about 20 minutes. Season with the salt and transfer to a warmed platter. Serve hot.

TURKEY MEATBALLS
WITH LEMON SAUCE

Serves 4 to 6

Making meatballs with turkey or chicken can be tricky because unlike beef, poultry dries out easily when it is overcooked by even a few seconds. There are two keys to keeping the meat moist during cooking. First, because breast meat toughens easily, it is best to use dark meat. Second, keep the heat low during cooking. In my family, a favourite accompaniment to these meatballs is Creamy Mashed Potatoes with Garlic (page 173).

2 SLICES WHITE BREAD, CRUSTS REMOVED

MILK, FOR SOAKING

2 TABLESPOONS EXTRA-VIRGIN OLIVE OIL

4 SHALLOTS, FINELY CHOPPED

450G MINCED TURKEY DARK MEAT

50G PANCETTA, FINELY CHOPPED (OPTIONAL)

1 SMALL EGG, BEATEN

25G FRESHLY GRATED PARMIGIANO-REGGIANO OR GRANA PADANO CHEESE

¼ TEASPOON FRESHLY GRATED NUTMEG

1 TEASPOON SEA SALT

FRESHLY GROUND BLACK PEPPER

60G PLAIN FLOUR

2 TABLESPOONS UNSALTED BUTTER

110ML DRY WHITE WINE

125ML CHICKEN STOCK (PAGE 214), OR AS NEEDED

FRESHLY SQUEEZED JUICE OF ½ LEMON

1. In a small bowl, cover the bread with milk until soaked; squeeze dry and set aside.

2. Warm 1 tablespoon of the olive oil in a small frying pan and sauté the shallots over medium heat until softened, about 3 minutes.

3. In a mixing bowl, combine the turkey, bread, sautéed shallots, pancetta (if using), egg, cheese, nutmeg, salt and pepper. Form a small meat patty and fry it to check for seasoning. Chill the mixture for at least an hour before forming into 2.5-cm meatballs. Just before cooking, dredge them lightly in flour and shake off excess.

4. In a frying pan, melt the butter with the remaining tablespoon olive oil. Sauté the meatballs over medium-low to medium heat in one layer, browning them gently all over. When an instant-read thermometer inserted into the centre registers 71.1°C, the meatballs are done, about 8 minutes. Transfer to a warm plate.

5. When all the meatballs are cooked, add the wine to the pan and scrape up any bits of meat. Stir in the chicken stock and simmer until a creamy sauce is formed, about 3 minutes. Strain through a sieve, and add salt and pepper to taste. Whisk in the lemon juice. Add the meatballs to the sauce and heat through gently over low heat, turning occasionally, about 2 minutes. Adjust for salt and pepper and serve.

7

MAIN DISHES:
MEAT

Economical cuts, stewed or braised in a rich bath fortified with wine or vinegar, are popular in Italian homes, as are veal, pork and grass-fed beef, cooked with aromatics in olive oil or sometimes butter, and thin, breaded fried cutlets. Roasted and grilled meats grace the family table as well, and lamb in particular is appreciated for its robust flavour and Christian symbolism. (The lamb on the shoulder of Christ the Good Shepherd represents a soul going home to God.) Each spring of my youth my parents went to rural Pennsylvania to buy milk-fed baby lamb for Easter. The trip recalled my mother's childhood in Sardinia, where, as all over Italy, a true baby lamb is not a day over six weeks. Delicate, buttery and fork-tender, it's much superior to ordinary spring lamb. Some of the recipes in this chapter are actually Italian-American, but there are also original and surprising dishes that are unknown except to the fortunate families of the home cooks who taught them to me.

MOIST PAN-FRIED PORK CHOPS
WITH CRUNCHY CRUMB AND FENNEL COATING

Serves 4

Here are my aunt Rita's delicious pork chops, moist inside with a crispy fennel crust. For best and most wholesome results, buy 'natural' pork. Industrially raised pork is injected with liquid, which interferes with proper browning. The secret to the success of these chops is to not overcook them; follow directions precisely for good results. The best accompaniments are Creamy Mashed Potatoes with Garlic (page 173) and Anna Amendolara Nurse's braised cabbage with garlic, pancetta and hot red pepper (see page 167).

10G BREADCRUMBS OR PANKO

2 TABLESPOONS FENNEL SEEDS

½ TEASPOON SEA SALT

FRESHLY GROUND BLACK PEPPER

½ TEASPOON EXTRA-VIRGIN OLIVE OIL FOR BRUSHING ON MEAT, PLUS 3 TABLESPOONS FOR FRYING

4 BONELESS PORK TOPLOIN CHOPS (100G), NO MORE THAN 2CM THICK

1. Preheat the oven to 90°C/200°F/gas mark ¼. Spread the breadcrumbs or panko on a baking tray and slide them onto the middle rack of the oven. Bake until faintly coloured but not at all brown, about 7 minutes. Warm the fennel seeds in a frying pan over medium-low heat until their aroma is released, about 2 minutes. Transfer to a spice mill and grind to a semi-fine texture; there should still be just the slightest roughness.

2. Combine the toasted breadcrumbs with the ground fennel seeds, salt and pepper to taste, and spread out on a piece of greaseproof paper. Pound the chops lightly on both sides to a thickness of 1cm. Blot both sides with kitchen paper. Brush the chops with the ½ teaspoon olive oil. Just before cooking, dredge the chops in the crumb mixture and press into the surface with the palm of your hand.

3. Warm a shallow 30-cm cast-iron frying pan or non-stick frying pan over medium heat. When a drop of water skitters on the surface, after about 4 minutes, pour in the 3 tablespoons olive oil. When it is sizzling hot, place the chops in the pan, pressing each with your fingers to provide immediate contact. Cook over medium heat until golden on the first side, about 2 minutes. Use a fish slice to flip the chops over and turn off the heat. Cover the pan tightly and allow the chops to rest until an instant-read meat thermometer inserted into the centre registers 54.4°C, about 3 minutes. Remove the cover and increase the heat to medium. Brown to crisp on both sides, about 2 minutes in total, using a spatula to carefully turn the meat to prevent the crispy coating from sticking to the pan surface. Transfer the chops to a warm platter, tent lightly with foil and leave to rest for 5 minutes before serving.

SAUTÉED SWEET PORK SAUSAGES
WITH ROASTED BLACK GRAPES

Serves 4

I learned to pair pork sausages and grapes in Umbria during the harvest when the wine grape is in abundance and quick and hearty dishes are prepared for the workers labouring in the vineyards. In the traditional recipe (see Note, below), the grapes are cooked in a cast-iron frying pan along with the sausages, but I've gotten into the habit of roasting the grapes separately, which sears and caramelises them and concentrates their flavours more. You can do this in a toaster oven rather than heating up a large oven for such a small amount of fruit. Whatever way you cook them, it's a lovely dish. You might serve it with Basic Polenta (page 217) and Anna Maria's Roasted Onions with Crumb Topping (page 172), followed by Warm Winter Greens Salad with Bacon Vinaigrette (page 64).

8 SWEET ITALIAN PORK SAUSAGES

125ML WATER

350G SEEDLESS BLACK OR RED GRAPES, STRIPPED FROM THEIR STEMS

COOKING OIL SPRAY OR OLIVE OIL

1. Use a sharp knife or fork to poke a few holes in the sausages before cooking them. Select a seasoned cast-iron frying pan or other heavy-bottomed pan. Put the sausages and the water in the frying pan and place over medium heat. When the water has evaporated and the sausages have begun to colour lightly, after about 12 minutes, reduce the heat to medium-low and continue to cook the sausages, pricking them occasionally to release excess fat, until they are browned all over and cooked through, about 20 minutes more. (Do not prick them too much, or they will dry out.)

2. For the grapes, preheat a toaster oven or an oven to 190°C. Wash and dry the grapes well. Oil them very lightly with cooking oil spray or toss them in a bowl with a touch of olive oil. Spread them out on the toaster oven tray or on a baking tray and roast until brown and bubbly, about 15 minutes. Note that they can burn easily because of their high sugar content, so keep an eye on them as they cook.

3. Transfer the sausages and grapes to a large warmed platter, leaving behind any fat, and serve immediately.

NOTE: If you would like to cook the grapes in the pan alongside the sausages, add them to the frying pan when the sausage cooking water has evaporated and the sausages have begun to colour lightly, after about 12 minutes. Proceed as directed for the remainder of the method.

ZIA RITA'S
STUFFED BEEF BRACIOLE
Serves 4

My aunt Rita Ghisu came from Cagliari. Her cooking is like her, elegant and refined – like these braciole stuffed with mortadella, pistachios, savoury crumbs and grated Parmigiano-Reggiano cheese. Use skirt steak or thin slices of silverside steak pounded to 5mm thick.

1.1KG SKIRT STEAK, 2CM THICK, PARTIALLY FROZEN

25G CHOPPED, TOASTED SHELLED PISTACHIOS

6 LARGE CLOVES GARLIC, CHOPPED

2 MEDIUM SHALLOTS, FINELY CHOPPED

5 TABLESPOONS CHOPPED FRESH FLAT-LEAF PARSLEY

6 TABLESPOONS FRESHLY GRATED PARMIGIANO-REGGIANO OR GRANA PADANO CHEESE

12 THIN SLICES MORTADELLA, OR PROSCIUTTO

4 TABLESPOONS EXTRA-VIRGIN OLIVE OIL

1 TABLESPOON UNSALTED BUTTER

2 800-G TINS CRUSHED ITALIAN PLUM TOMATOES

2 TEASPOONS SEA SALT

250ML GOOD-QUALITY DRY RED WINE

FRESHLY GROUND BLACK PEPPER

COTTON BUTCHER'S TWINE OR STRONG COCKTAIL STICKS

1. Butterfly the steak and pound it to 5mm thick. Place the steak cut-side up with the grain parallel to the edge of your work surface. Cut into 12 pieces, each 7.5 x 10cm. Distribute the pistachios, garlic, shallots, parsley and grated cheese over each piece of steak. Then roll a slice of mortadella into a cigar shape and place it in the centre of each piece of meat so that it lies in the same direction as the grain. Roll up each bundle of meat tightly and tie it securely with butcher's twine. Alternatively, use cocktail sticks to keep the rolls closed. The rolls should be neither overly tight nor overly loose.

2. In a cast-iron casserole dish that is large enough to accommodate all the braciole at once without crowding, warm the olive oil and butter together. When it is hot enough to sear the meat, slip the braciole into the pan. If the pan is not large enough, sear in two batches. Brown the braciole on all sides over medium-high heat, about 15 minutes. Lower the heat to medium-low and add the tomatoes and salt to the pan. Partially cover and simmer over the lowest heat so that barely a bubble breaks the surface, about 1 hour. Add the wine and continue to simmer until the meat is very tender, about 2½ hours.

3. Add pepper to taste and check for seasoning. Allow the braciole to settle for 15 minutes before serving. Remove the string or cocktail sticks. Serve the sauce over freshly cooked polenta, rice, macaroni or strand-type pasta. Serve the braciole separately as a second course.

NONNA VERA'S
TENDER AND CRUNCHY BEEF MEDALLIONS

Serves 4

I learned this wonderful recipe from my Italian friend Anna Maria Erenbourg Weld. It is a recipe from her grandmother, Vera Ehrenbourg D'Angara. Nonna Vera always served them with sweet and sour carrots (page 164). Keep in mind that because the medallions (patties) have a crunchy surface but remain tender and juicy within, they should be neither undercooked nor overcooked. For best results, follow the directions carefully.

MILK

2 SLICES STALE ARTISAN BREAD, CRUSTS REMOVED, SHREDDED, YIELDING 50G

50G BREADCRUMBS FOR COATING MEAT PATTIES, PLUS 5G

3 TABLESPOONS EXTRA-VIRGIN OLIVE OIL

1 SMALL ONION, FINELY CHOPPED

30G PLAIN FLOUR

1 EXTRA-LARGE EGG

1 TEASPOON SEA SALT, PLUS MORE FOR SPRINKLING

¼ TEASPOON FRESHLY GROUND BLACK PEPPER

450G MINCED LEAN ORGANIC BEEF

PURE OLIVE OIL, FOR FRYING

1. In a small bowl, pour enough milk to cover the shredded bread. When completely soaked, squeeze the milk out but keep the bread moist. Discard the milk. Spread the 50g of breadcrumbs on a large piece of greaseproof paper.

2. In a large frying pan, warm the extra-virgin olive oil. Add the onion and sauté until softened, about 4 minutes. Sprinkle on the flour and stir. When the flour has absorbed the oil and coated the onions, after about 3 minutes, let the mixture cool.

3. In a mixing bowl, beat the egg with the salt and pepper. Add the minced beef, the 5g breadcrumbs, onions and bread, crumbled. Wet your hands and blend the mixture very thoroughly. Form patties about 5cm in diameter and 5mm thick resembling large, round coins. Pat the sides to create a straight coin-like edge rather than a sloped edge. Use a knife to score each medallion with a tic-tac-toe on both sides, (this will allow the patties to form a lovely crunchy surface while the centre remains moist). Just before frying, dredge in breadcrumbs, shaking off excess.

4. Wipe out your frying pan. Pour in enough olive oil to reach halfway up the sides of the patties. Warm the oil over medium heat. When it is sizzling hot, slip the patties in, allowing plenty of room around each for proper searing. Cook over medium heat until nicely browned and crunchy on the surface, about 15 minutes. Resist the temptation to press down on the patties as they cook; doing this will make the patties dry and hard. Drain on kitchen paper and sprinkle lightly with salt while hot.

CLASSIC MEATBALLS

Serves 8

These savoury little delicacies are typically browned in oil, then transferred to a pot of tomato sauce to finish cooking. But they can also be served 'nude', meaning without sauce. In summer, I like to impale them on sturdy twigs of fresh rosemary after they are cooked and serve them as appetisers.

50G CUBED STALE WHITE BREAD, CRUSTS REMOVED (ABOUT 2 SLICES)

125ML MILK OR TASTY MEAT STOCK (PAGE 213)

450G LEAN MINCED BEEF

225G LEAN MINCED PORK

50G PROSCIUTTO, FINELY CHOPPED

1 SMALL ONION, GRATED ON THE LARGE OVAL HOLES OF A BOX GRATER

1 FRESH PLUM TOMATO, PEELED, DESEEDED AND FINELY CHOPPED

3 GARLIC CLOVES, GRATED

2 TEASPOONS CHOPPED FRESH MARJORAM, OR 1 TEASPOON CRUMBLED DRIED MARJORAM

1 EXTRA-LARGE EGG, LIGHTLY BEATEN

2 TEASPOONS SEA SALT, PLUS MORE TO TASTE

FRESHLY GROUND BLACK PEPPER

PURE OLIVE OIL, FOR FRYING

PLAIN FLOUR, FOR DREDGING

1. Put the bread in a small bowl and add the milk or stock. When the bread is softened thoroughly, squeeze dry, discarding the liquid, and place it in a bowl. Add the minced meats, prosciutto, onion, tomato, garlic, marjoram, egg, 2 teaspoons salt and pepper to taste. Using your hands, blend the mixture well. Make a small patty and fry it to check for seasoning. Form into walnut-size meatballs.

2. Pour the oil to a depth of 1cm into a large, wide frying pan and place over medium heat. Spread the flour onto an ample sheet of greaseproof paper. Lightly dredge as many meatballs as you will fry in the first batch. When the oil is hot enough to make the meatballs sizzle upon contact, slip them into the pan one at a time, being careful not to crowd the pan. Fry over medium heat until nicely browned all over and cooked through, about 10 minutes.

3. Using tongs or a slotted fish slice, transfer to kitchen paper to drain, then place on a platter and keep warm. Taste for salt and, if necessary, sprinkle salt sparingly over the meatballs. Serve hot or warm.

TOMATO SAUCE VARIATION: To prepare the meatballs in tomato sauce, prepare a double recipe of any of the meatless tomato sauces in chapter 2. Cook the meatballs as directed, then simmer together with the sauce over low heat for 20 minutes before serving.

JUICY MEAT LOAF
WITH TOMATO AND RED WINE GLAZE

Serves 8

Italian meat loaf is delicately seasoned and almost always made with several kinds of meat. I've gotten into the habit of working a little finely chopped fresh tomato into the mixture, which helps to keep it moist. Towards the end of cooking, the pan juices are fortified with tomato puree and wine to form a delicious sauce. Serve this succulent meat loaf for dinner, or leftover at room temperature; it is equally good hot or cold.

6 SLICES STALE WHITE BREAD WITH CRUSTS REMOVED, SHREDDED

MILK OR TASTY MEAT STOCK (PAGE 213)

2 TABLESPOONS OLIVE OIL

2 ONIONS, FINELY CHOPPED

2 LARGE GARLIC CLOVES, FINELY CHOPPED

3 TABLESPOONS BREADCRUMBS

3 LARGE EGGS, BEATEN

2 TEASPOONS SEA SALT

1½ TEASPOONS FRESHLY GROUND BLACK PEPPER

50G FRESHLY GRATED PARMIGIANO-REGGIANO OR GRANA PADANO CHEESE

6 TABLESPOONS FINELY CHOPPED FRESH FLAT-LEAF PARSLEY

1 TABLESPOON FINELY CHOPPED FRESH THYME, OR 2 TEASPOONS CRUSHED DRIED THYME

1.3KG MIXED LEAN MINCED BEEF AND PORK, OR 1.3KG LEAN MINCED BEEF

110G SOPRESSATA, FINELY CHOPPED

2 LARGE, FIRM, FRESH TOMATOES, PEELED, DESEEDED AND FINELY CHOPPED

6 TABLESPOONS TASTY MEAT STOCK (PAGE 213) OR WATER

125ML GOOD-QUALITY DRY RED WINE

750ML TOMATO SAUCE (PASSATA)

1. Preheat the oven to 180°C/350°F/gas mark 4. Soak the bread in enough milk or stock to cover. Squeeze it dry and discard the liquid. Shred and set aside.

2. In a frying pan, warm the olive oil and sauté the onion and garlic over medium heat until soft, about 7 minutes; cool.

3. In the meantime, scatter the breadcrumbs on an approximate 30.5 x 45.5-cm work surface. Grease a 23 x 33-cm baking dish.

4. In an ample mixing bowl, lightly beat the eggs with the salt, pepper, grated cheese, parsley and thyme. Add the meat(s), soppressata, shredded bread, sautéed onion and finely chopped tomato. Wet your hands and thoroughly blend all the ingredients together. Spread the meat mixture on the breadcrumb-covered work surface, using your hands to form a typical long and narrow log-shaped loaf. Place the meat loaf in the baking dish and sprinkle 3 tablespoons of the stock or water around it.

5. Slide the meat loaf onto the middle rack of the oven and bake for 50 minutes, or until an instant-read meat thermometer registers at 71.1°C, adding the remaining stock or water after 15 minutes. Baste several times during baking with the dish juices, adding a little more water if the juices seem to be drying up; no more than a tablespoon or two, if any, should be necessary. There should be sufficient juice in the baking dish to keep the meat loaf moist and to guarantee pan juices when it is done. Fifteen minutes before the meat is cooked, add the wine to the dish and pour the tomato sauce over the top to glaze the surface. When done, remove the meat loaf from the oven, tent with foil and leave to rest for 15 minutes. Pass the sauce and drippings that have formed in the dish through a sieve into a saucepan, and heat through over low heat, stirring to blend. Taste and adjust for seasoning.

6. Cut the meat loaf into 2-cm-thick slices. Overlap them on a serving platter or individual plates. Moisten with the sauce and serve, passing more sauce at the table.

LONG-SIMMERED BEEF STEW
WITH CLOVES AND RED WINE

Serves 4

Called *stracotto* in Italian, this richly flavoured stew is often the mainstay of Sunday supper. It produces plenty of juices, which also makes it ideal to serve with bread, steaming polenta (see page 217), or mashed potatoes. The cooking method is much in the style of the famous beef stew of Burgundy, resulting in butter-tender meat and an intoxicatingly rich, winey sauce – excellent cold-weather food.

1.3KG STEWING BEEF, TRIMMED OF EXCESS FAT AND CUBED

5 TABLESPOONS EXTRA-VIRGIN OLIVE OIL

110G PORK FATBACK, CUT INTO MATCHSTICK STRIPS

2 ONIONS, CHOPPED

5 LARGE GARLIC CLOVES, SMASHED

2 BAY LEAVES

1 TEASPOON FINELY CHOPPED FRESH MARJORAM, OR ½ TEASPOON CRUMBLED DRIED MARJORAM

½ TEASPOON GROUND CLOVES

3 CARROTS, CUT INTO DICE

7.5-CM STRIP OF LEMON ZEST

1½ TEASPOONS SEA SALT, OR TO TASTE

FRESHLY GROUND BLACK PEPPER

3 TABLESPOONS PLAIN FLOUR

3 TABLESPOONS TOMATO PURÉE

175ML GOOD-QUALITY, FULL-BODIED DRY RED WINE, SUCH AS CHIANTI

1. Preheat the oven to 230°C/450°F/gas mark 8. Blot the meat well with kitchen paper.

2. In a cast-iron casserole dish with a wide surface, warm 3 tablespoons of the olive oil over medium heat and add the fatback; sauté until lightly browned, 2 to 3 minutes. Use a slotted spoon to transfer it to a dish and set aside. Add the beef in two batches to the pan and brown it on all sides, about 12 minutes. Transfer the beef to the dish with the fatback. Wipe the dish with kitchen paper.

3. Add 2 more tablespoons olive oil to the dish and stir in the onion, garlic, bay leaves, marjoram, cloves, carrots and lemon zest. Sauté until lightly coloured and aromatic, about 6 minutes. Return the beef and the fat back to the dish, season with salt and pepper and stir. Sprinkle the flour over the meat. Stir in the tomato purée mixed with a little water, then the wine and enough water to barely cover the meat. Cover and cook over low heat until the meat is tender, about 2 hours. Add water as needed to prevent the meat from drying out and to ensure plenty of juices. Keep the liquid at half the height of the meat. Stir occasionally.

4. When the meat is done, remove the bay leaves and lemon zest. Taste for seasoning and serve.

VEAL STEW
WITH LEMON, ROSEMARY AND PINE NUT SAUCE

Serves 4

This is one of my mother's stew recipes, invented one night when there were veal steaks in our refrigerator needing to be cooked. It was designed for an economy cut of veal that will stand up to lengthy cooking; a shoulder cut is ideal. Adding pine nuts provides interesting texture and a nutty flavour. Slow braising produces enough gravy for 225g of fresh egg noodles, Saffron Fregula (page 88), or a heap of Creamy Mashed Potatoes with Garlic (page 173).

2.5-CM-THICK BONELESS VEAL SHOULDER STEAKS (350G EACH)

5 TABLESPOONS PLAIN FLOUR

3 TABLESPOONS UNSALTED BUTTER

2 TABLESPOONS EXTRA-VIRGIN OLIVE OIL

150ML GOOD-QUALITY DRY WHITE WINE

1 TABLESPOON FRESH ROSEMARY, OR 1 TEASPOON CRUSHED DRIED ROSEMARY

500ML CHICKEN STOCK (PAGE 214)

3 5-CM STRIPS LEMON PEEL, ZEST ONLY

½ TEASPOON SALT, OR TO TASTE

2 TABLESPOONS COARSELY CHOPPED, LIGHTLY TOASTED PINE NUTS

½ TEASPOON FRESHLY GROUND WHITE OR BLACK PEPPER

1. Trim excess fat from the veal and cut each steak in half. If there is bone, include it in the dish, as it will add flavour to the sauce and can be sucked for the marrow like a miniature osso bucco. Spread the flour on a piece of greaseproof paper.

2. Heat half of the butter and olive oil together in a deep frying pan until sizzling hot. Dredge half of the veal in the flour and slip into the pan. Brown over moderately high heat, turning once, until nicely coloured on both sides, about 15 minutes. Transfer to a platter and repeat with the remaining butter, oil and veal, as above.

3. Add the wine and rosemary to the pan and cook, stirring with a wooden spoon, until the wine evaporates, about 1 minute. Stir in about 75ml of the stock. Return the veal to the pan in a single layer, cover and simmer over moderately low heat until the stock is absorbed, about 10 minutes. Stir in 60-ml measurements of stock at 10-minute intervals, or as needed, to keep the meat moist.

4. After 1 hour, add the lemon zest. Continue to cook the veal over low heat, covered, until tender, another 45 to 60 minutes. Continue to add the remaining stock at 10-minute intervals as necessary. Stir in the salt and pine nuts 15 minutes before the meat is done. Stir in the pepper and serve.

AHEAD-OF-TIME NOTE: The stew can be refrigerated for up to 3 days. Rewarm over low heat, stirring in about 60ml extra chicken stock.

ROMAN BRAISED LAMB
WITH WHITE WINE AND ARTICHOKES

Serves 4

Here is a dish adapted from a recipe given to me by my Swedish-born friend, Clarisse Schiller, who has lived in Italy for most of her life. She learned how to cook the lusty dishes of the Roman countryside from her mother-in-law, and passed many of them on to me. I especially like this one because I am fond of the combination of lamb and artichokes. The artichokes should be fresh and once they are cleaned, the rest of the preparation is quite simple. The thick, aromatic gravy calls for serving the stew with plenty of sturdy bread, polenta or crostini. Offer good dry red wine at the table, too.

ZEST OF 1 LEMON AND JUICE OF 2 LEMONS

6 FRESH MEDIUM ARTICHOKES, OR 10 FRESH BABY ARTICHOKES

900G (TRIMMED WEIGHT) LAMB SHOULDER OR OTHER STEWING CUT OF LAMB, INCLUDING SOME BONE

60G PLAIN FLOUR

3 TABLESPOONS EXTRA-VIRGIN OLIVE OIL

3 LARGE GARLIC CLOVES, CRUSHED

1 CARROT, SHREDDED ON THE LARGE

HOLES OF A BOX GRATER

¾ TEASPOON SEA SALT, OR TO TASTE

125ML DRY WHITE WINE

350ML CHICKEN STOCK, PLUS MORE IF NEEDED (PAGE 214)

THREE 15-CM SPRIGS FRESH DILL, OR 3 TABLESPOONS FINELY CHOPPED FRESH FENNEL FRONDS

FRESHLY GROUND BLACK PEPPER

1. Add about 15cm of water to a large glass or ceramic bowl, then squeeze the juice of one of the lemons into it. Trim a thin slice from the bottom of the stem of each artichoke. Pare off all the dark green skin on the stem. With one hand, pull off the tough outer leaves until you reach leaves with tender white areas at their base. Using a serrated knife, cut off the upper dark green part of the inner leaves; leave the light base. (If you decide to use baby artichokes, there will be fewer tough outer leaves to remove.) Cut the artichoke in half lengthways and, with a small knife, cut out the hairy choke and any other tough inner purple leaves. As each artichoke is finished, immediately put it in the lemon water to prevent it from turning brown. (Once cleaned, the artichokes can remain in the lemon water in the fridge for up to 24 hours.) When all of the artichokes have been trimmed, drain them, cut each half in half again, and pat dry. Place each artichoke half, cut-side down, on a chopping board and cut into quarters lengthways. Cook the sliced artichoke hearts in boiling water to cover for 10 minutes. Drain and set aside.

2. Trim the excess fat from the lamb, but leave the bones, which will add to the flavour of the stew. Cut the meat into approximate 4-cm pieces. Place the lamb in

a bowl with 5cm of cold water to cover and the remaining lemon juice. Use your hands to squeeze out excess blood, then leave it to soak for 30 minutes. Drain the meat, rinse and pat thoroughly dry with clean tea towels.

3. Scatter the lemon zest on a piece of greaseproof paper the size of a chopping board, and roll the meat in it. Spread the meat out in a single layer. Sprinkle it lightly with the flour and shake off any excess.

4. In a large, heavy frying pan or cast-iron casserole dish, warm the olive oil over medium heat and add the lamb. Brown nicely all over, about 12 minutes. Add the garlic, carrot and salt. Stir in the wine. Cook to evaporate, about 2 minutes. Cover halfway with the stock, reduce the heat to low, partially cover and cook, adding more stock a little at a time as needed, until the lamb is tender, about 1¼ hours, depending on the cut of the meat. Check the pan frequently to prevent the meat from drying out. When the meat is almost done, add the artichoke hearts and cover. Cook over low heat until the artichoke hearts are tender and the flavours of all the ingredients marry, another 10 to 15 minutes. Stir in the dill or fennel and season with pepper.

8

MAIN DISHES:
SEAFOOD

'*Mangiamo il pesce!*' – 'Let's have fish!' – my cousins cried whenever I visited them in Cagliari. Whether cooked at home or eaten at a restaurant near the beach, a seafood meal was a treat. This wasn't always the case in Sardinia, which is a lush garden in the middle of the sea. If you were to have visited there before Mussolini's time, before the malaria-infested swamps along the coastline were drained, you wouldn't have gone anywhere near the sea. But the island's seafood was astonishingly good, prepared simply with the fragrant local olive oil and perhaps saffron, wild marjoram and wild fennel. Many such memories are tucked away in the happy reaches of my mind. I know only too well how special these seafood dinners were, and now how rare. Today, even in Italy, most fish is farmed because some species are overfished and others tainted by high levels of mercury. Nevertheless, many excellent dishes can be made with what is available. The Italian way with seafood is to keep it simple, such as the dishes included here.

OVEN-FRIED TILAPIA
WITH FENNEL CRUST

Serves 4

The Mediterranean combination of fish and fennel is a marriage made in heaven, especially in this crunchy-crusted tilapia creation I originally invented for schoolchildren. Once introduced to their repertoire, it became one of the all-time favourites on the lunch menu – for children and adults alike, even among the less sophisticated eaters who thought they didn't like fish.

60G BREADCRUMBS OR PANKO

1 TEASPOON FRESHLY, FINELY GROUND FENNEL SEEDS

½ TEASPOON CRUSHED DRIED THYME

250ML EXTRA-VIRGIN OLIVE OIL

4 FRESH TILAPIA FILLETS (ABOUT 900G), EACH CUT DOWN THE MIDDLE AND SLICED INTO A TOTAL OF 6 PIECES

4 TABLESPOONS DIJON MUSTARD

1. Preheat an oven to 90°C/200°F/gas mark ¼. Spread the breadcrumbs out on a baking tray and slide them onto the middle rack of the oven. Bake until faintly coloured but not at all brown, about 7 minutes. Remove and cool.

2. Increase the oven temperature to 180°C/350°F/gas mark 4. Spray a baking tray with cooking spray.

3. In a shallow bowl, combine the breadcrumbs with the herbs and the olive oil. Using a pastry brush, paint the fish pieces with a thin film of the mustard. Then coat each piece with the breadcrumb mixture and transfer to the baking tray, leaving plenty of room between each piece for heat to circulate around it.

4. Bake until cooked through but still moist and tender, about 10 minutes. (Note: cooking time is accurate for small, cut-up fillet pieces. For larger pieces, cook longer.) Arrange 6 pieces of the fillets on each individual plate and serve at once.

LUCIANO ERENBOURG'S PAN-FRIED
FISH FILLETS WITH CRISPY SAGE LEAVES

Serves 4

This elegantly simple recipe was discovered by my friend's brother, Luciano Erenbourg, during a summer in his Otranto home on the Adriatic. There, the gilt-head bream is used for sautéing in this manner, but outside of Italy we can substitute other firm-fleshed fish. Tilapia is very accessible and inexpensive, so it is my fish fillet of choice for this method.

4 FRESH TILAPIA FILLETS (ABOUT 900G TOTAL)

SEA SALT AND FRESHLY GROUND BLACK OR WHITE PEPPER

3 TABLESPOONS EXTRA-VIRGIN OLIVE OIL

20 MEDIUM-SIZE FRESH SAGE LEAVES

1. Season the fish with salt and pepper on both sides.

2. Warm a wide, shallow cast-iron frying pan over medium-high heat. When a drop of water skitters on the surface, after about 3 minutes, add the olive oil. Tilt the pan to coat the base evenly and place the sage leaves on the base of the pan. Heat until the oil is almost smoking, about 30 seconds.

3. Lay the fish fillets on top of the sage leaves. If the pan is not large enough to accommodate all the fillets, cook them in two batches. Sear until lightly browned on the bottom, about 3 minutes. Flip each piece over. Reduce the heat to medium and sear until done but still moist, about 2 minutes. Transfer the cooked fillets to a warm plate and repeat the whole process for the second batch, placing fresh sage leaves under each as before. Serve at once.

BARON GIUSEPPE ROSSO'S
FRESH TUNA WITH ONION COMPOTE

Serves 4

When I met Giusepppe Rosso while on a tour of Sicily's olive oil estates, he lamented the erosion of traditional cooking in his region, where his ancestors have produced oil from Tonda Iblea olive groves dating back to the 14th century. This is one of the local dishes his cook made using his prized Villa Zottopera organic oil. The caramelised sweet onions, bathed in tomato and fortified with wine, serve as a bed for the seared tuna steaks. The same treatment given to tuna can be applied to other firm-fleshed fish steaks, including swordfish, cod and halibut.

4 TUNA FILLETS OR STEAKS
(ABOUT 700G TOTAL)

SEA SALT AND FRESHLY GROUND
BLACK PEPPER

4 TABLESPOONS EXTRA-VIRGIN OLIVE OIL,
PREFERABLY SICILIAN

125ML DRY WHITE WINE (PREFERABLY
SICILIAN)

2 LARGE WHITE (SWEET) ONIONS,
QUARTERED AND SLICED THIN

1½ TEASPOONS FINELY CHOPPED FRESH
OREGANO, OR 1 TEASPOON DRIED
OREGANO

300G CHOPPED FRESH RIPE TOMATOES

1. Use kitchen paper to dry the tuna fillets or steaks well and season with salt.

2. Select a seasoned cast-iron frying pan or other non-stick frying pan that is large enough to accommodate all the fish at once. If you don't have a large enough pan, sear the fish in smaller batches. Over medium-high heat, pour half of the olive oil in the pan and when it is hot, add the tuna. Sauté the steaks quickly over medium-high heat to sear the surface, about 2 minutes on each side, or until browned lightly on both sides and rare in the middle. Transfer to a platter. Add the wine to the pan and deglaze over medium heat. Pour over the tuna steaks and set aside, keeping the tuna warm.

3. Warm the remaining oil in the same pan over medium heat. Add the onions and oregano to the pan and sauté over medium-low heat until they are thoroughly softened and nicely coloured, about 12 minutes, stirring occasionally for even cooking. Add the chopped tomatoes and simmer over medium heat, stirring occasionally, until the excess liquid evaporates, about 10 minutes. Taste for salt.

4. Return the tuna and its juices to the pan and heat through to finish cooking to taste, being careful not to overcook it. The tuna should be cooked medium to medium-rare and should remain moist and tender inside. Serve at once.

PAN-FRIED TROUT
WITH WHITE WINE AND CAPER SAUCE

Serves 4

When I buy fresh trout in the market, I often cook it this way, a method I learned from a Roman friend. Freshwater fish often needs a flavour boost, accomplished here simply with capers and wine. Newcomers to my table, even the young and the fish-wary, are always delighted with this dish. Have the fishmonger gut and clean the fish and remove the heads so that you will have four fillets with the skin remaining on one side. If increasing the recipe yield, sauté the fillets in batches to avoid overcrowding them in the frying pan.

4 BONELESS TROUT FILLET HALVES, SKIN ON (ABOUT 700G TOTAL)

125G PLAIN FLOUR

SEA SALT AND FRESHLY GROUND WHITE OR BLACK PEPPER

4 TABLESPOONS UNSALTED BUTTER

4 TABLESPOONS EXTRA-VIRGIN OLIVE OIL

4 TABLESPOONS SMALL CAPERS, DRAINED

120ML DRY WHITE WINE

1. Pat the fish dry with kitchen paper. This step is very important in order to sauté them properly.

2. Place a large piece of greaseproof paper on your work surface and measure the flour onto it. Sprinkle with salt and pepper, then spread the flour out.

3. In a large frying pan, melt the butter with the oil over medium heat until it is hot enough to make the fish sizzle. Meanwhile, lightly dredge the trout in the flour. Dredging must be done at the last minute to assure a crisp coating.

4. Slip the trout, skin-side down, into the pan. Do this in batches to ensure plenty of room around each fish for proper sautéing. Pan-fry until the coating is brown, about 3 minutes. Turn the trout over and pan-fry until opaque in the centre, about 2 minutes. Transfer the trout to a warm platter.

5. Reduce the heat to medium-low and add the capers and wine to the pan. Stir to scrape up any browned bits from the base of the pan. Cook until the alcohol has evaporated, about 2 minutes. Season with salt. Pour the sauce over the trout fillets and serve at once.

GRILLED WHOLE FISH
IN THE MANNER OF MURANO

Serves 4

The residents of the tiny island of Murano in the Venice lagoon believe that the best way to cook fish is to simply grill or fry it in order not to hamper its pleasureable natural flavour. Here, lemon in company with seafood is considered the height of bad taste since, historically, it was used to disguise stinking fish. Vinegar or white wine and a fresh herb or two is usually all that a Venetian will tolerate. Slices of grilled polenta (see page 217), drizzled with extra-virgin olive oil, make a good accompaniment.

4 PORGIES, STRIPED BASS OR STRIPED MULLETS, ABOUT 700G EACH, GUTTED AND SCALED

SEA SALT

8 BAY LEAVES

EXTRA-VIRGIN OLIVE OIL

125ML WHITE WINE VINEGAR

FRESHLY GROUND PEPPER, PREFERABLY WHITE

1. Preheat the grill. Alternatively, if cooking on a barbecue, prepare a fire and let the wood or coals burn to a white heat. If using the grill, you will want to place the fish on a preheated rack over the grill tray so that the heat can circulate on all sides of the fish as it cooks; if cooking over a barbecue, you will want to place the fish between two racks, or in a fish 'cage', so that they may be turned over easily and without breaking midway through cooking.

2. Rinse the fish and dry well with kitchen paper. Lightly sprinkle the cavity of each fish with salt, then stuff 2 bay leaves into each. Massage olive oil liberally on both sides of the fish, then sprinkle on half of the vinegar.

3. If grilling, place the fish on the preheated rack about 13cm under the heat source. Cook until the fish are golden and crisp on the outside, about 10 minutes. Remove the tray from under the grill, turn the fish over, sprinkle with the remaining vinegar and slide the tray under the grill again. Cook for an additional 8 minutes. If cooking over a barbecue, flip over the fish in the racks or cage when the skin is crisp, and cook on the reverse side until done, a total of about 15 minutes. When done, the fish should be opaque throughout when tested with the tip of a knife, and golden on the surface.

4. Discard the bay leaves and season the fish with salt and pepper. Serve at once.

GARLICKY
PAN-ROASTED PRAWNS

Serves 4

Here is one of the easiest and most popular ways for cooking prawns in Italy and throughout the Mediterranean. Good Italian bread should always be served with this dish for soaking up the delicious sauce.

450G LARGE PRAWNS, PEELED

125ML EXTRA-VIRGIN OLIVE OIL

4 LARGE GARLIC CLOVES, CUT INTO SMALL PIECES

PINCH RED PEPPER FLAKES, OR 1 OR 2 WHOLE DRIED PEPERONCINI (HOT PEPPERS)

60ML GOOD-QUALITY DRY WHITE WINE

2 TABLESPOONS CHOPPED FRESH FLAT-LEAF PARSLEY

1 LOAF CRUSTY ARTISAN BREAD, SLICED

1. Remove the dark intestinal veins from the prawns. As you do, make each cut deep enough to butterfly the prawns so they can be opened flat, like a book. Rinse under cold running water, drain and dry thoroughly with a cotton tea towel.

2. In a large frying pan, warm the oil over medium heat. Add the garlic and red pepper flakes or whole pepper and sauté gently until the garlic has softened but not browned, about 2 minutes. Add the prawns, placing them opened flat on the base of the pan so they do not curl too much; sauté, turning once, until they are opaque, about 2 minutes on each side. Add the wine, stir, and cook for an additional 30 seconds to allow the alcohol to evaporate. Remove the whole pepper, if using. Sprinkle with the parsley and serve immediately. Pass the bread at the table.

BAKED PRAWNS
WITH CRUNCHY CRUMB TOPPING

Serves 4

I learned this recipe from Anna Amendolara Nurse, one of the best home cooks I know. It is probably one of my favourite prawn dishes of all for its garlicky flavour and pleasant, crunchy topping (the Italians call a baked dish with a crunchy bread topping *gratinate*). It is often one of the seven seafood courses Anna makes for *la vigilia*, the traditional feast of seven fishes on Christmas Eve, because it so easy to make and so festive. You can make the topping in advance and keep it, covered and chilled, for up to a week.

700G LARGE PRAWNS, PEELED AND DEVEINED

6 TABLESPOONS EXTRA-VIRGIN OLIVE OIL, PLUS MORE FOR GREASING

1 LARGE GARLIC CLOVE, CRUSHED

2 TEASPOONS FINELY CHOPPED FRESH OREGANO OR 1 TEASPOON DRIED

½ TEASPOON RED PEPPER FLAKES

SEA SALT

40G PANKO OR PLAIN WHITE BREADCRUMBS

3 TABLESPOONS CHOPPED FRESH FLAT-LEAF PARSLEY

4 LEMON WEDGES (OPTIONAL)

1. Preheat the oven to 200°C/400°F/gas mark 6. Using a paring knife, make a cut down the back side of each prawn so that it can lie flat like a book with the tail end standing straight up like a handle.

2. In a bowl, combine the olive oil, garlic, oregano, red pepper flakes, salt, Panko or breadcrumbs and parsley.

3. Select a baking dish large enough to accommodate the prawns without crowding. Grease lightly with olive oil. Arrange the prawns inside, tail facing upwards. Sprinkle the breadcrumb mixture over the prawns.

4. Slide the baking dish on the middle rack of the oven. Cook without disturbing the prawns until the crumbs become brown, 10–12 minutes. Serve at once, with the lemon wedges, if desired.

'ANGRY' LOBSTER
BRAISED IN TOMATO SAUCE

Serves 4

This fiery Roman dish has come to be known as 'Lobster fra Diavolo', loosely translated as lobster 'in company with the devil'. The recipe is elementary, but perhaps it will serve as an encouragement to those who never deviate from eating their lobster boiled with drawn butter. Be sure to have good bread at the table for soaking up the splendid sauce.

4 LIVE LOBSTERS 600G EACH)

6 TABLESPOONS EXTRA-VIRGIN OLIVE OIL

8 LARGE GARLIC CLOVES, CRUSHED

½ TEASPOON RED PEPPER FLAKES

4 TABLESPOONS CHOPPED FRESH FLAT-LEAF PARSLEY

½ TEASPOON CRUSHED DRIED OREGANO

675G DRAINED TINNED ITALIAN PLUM TOMATOES, DESEEDED AND CHOPPED, OR 450G VINE-RIPENED PLUM TOMATOES, PEELED, DESEEDED AND CHOPPED

½ TEASPOON SALT, OR TO TASTE

1. Rinse the lobsters in cold water. Kill them humanely in the following way: place a sharp chef's knife at the point where the body and the head meet on the top of the carapace and quickly drive in the point to sever the spinal cord. Remove the rubber bands that bind the claws. Using the chef's knife, split the lobsters in half lengthways and pull out the black vein that runs the length of the body. Split each piece in half again crossways and crack the claws.

2. In a very large frying pan, warm the olive oil with the garlic over low heat until the garlic is golden but not browned, about 2 minutes. Stir in the red pepper flakes, parsley and oregano and sauté for 1 minute. Increase the heat to medium-low and add the lobsters to the pan. Sauté on all sides, stirring often, until the shells turn red and the meat begins to become opaque. Add the tomatoes and salt, partially cover and simmer gently until thickened, about 25 minutes. Remove from the heat and serve.

MUSSELS 'PEPPETEDDA'

Serves 4

Here is another seafood recipe from Puglia, my father's home region on the Adriatic coast. *Peppetedda* means 'peppery' in Pugliese dialect, referring to the hot paprika used. I tasted this dish when I travelled to Puglia for the first time to discover my paternal family's roots. Like most fare of the region, it is boldly flavoured and simple in its execution. Remember to only buy mussels that are tightly closed.

2.75KG FRESH, MEDIUM-SIZE MUSSELS

4 TABLESPOONS EXTRA-VIRGIN OLIVE OIL

2 ONIONS, FINELY CHOPPED

3 LARGE GARLIC CLOVES, CUT INTO SMALL PIECES

3 TABLESPOONS CHOPPED FRESH FLAT-LEAF PARSLEY

2 TEASPOONS CHOPPED FRESH THYME, OR 1 TEASPOON DRIED THYME

1 BAY LEAF

200G FRESH OR TINNED VINE-RIPENED TOMATOES, PEELED, CHOPPED AND DRAINED

1 TEASPOON HOT PAPRIKA, OR 1 TEASPOON SWEET PAPRIKA AND GENEROUS PINCH RED PEPPER FLAKES

350ML GOOD-QUALITY DRY WHITE WINE

LOAF OF CRUSTY ARTISAN BREAD, SLICED

1. With a very stiff brush, scrub the mussels well. Pull or cut off their beards. Use a small sharp knife to scrape off any barnacles. Wash them under cold running water to remove any traces of sand. Place the mussels in a large bowl with enough cold water to cover to cleanse them of any sand, soaking for 1 to 3 hours. Rinse again, discarding any that open or whose shells are not very tightly shut.

2. In a heavy cast-iron casserole dish large enough to easily accommodate the mussels, warm the olive oil. Add the onion and garlic and sauté over medium heat until the onion wilts, about 4 minutes. Add the parsley, thyme and bay leaf and continue to sauté for another few minutes until the onion is transparent. Add the tomatoes and the hot paprika or sweet paprika and red pepper flakes; simmer over medium heat until the sauce has thickened, about 7 minutes. Add the mussels and toss them with the sauce in the pan. Pour in the wine. Cover tightly and bring to the boil over medium-high heat. Lower the heat and simmer 2 to 3 minutes more, or until the mussels are fully open. Remove from the heat.

3. Discard any unopened mussels and divide the rest among 4 shallow bowls. Use a large spoon or ladle to spoon the mussel stock over each bowl, trying not to stir up the bottom, which may contain errant sand. Serve with plenty of bread.

9

FOR THE LOVE OF VEGETABLES:
VEGETARIAN MAIN COURSES AND
VEGETABLE SIDE DISHES

For many Italians, especially those south of Rome, eating meat had been a privilege of the wealthy until modern times. Grains, cheese and vegetables have been the bedrock of their diet, and for good reasons. The climate is temperate, often with long growing seasons, and those staples keep well without refrigeration. Italy was slow to industrialise, which had two effects. It delayed the arrival of kitchen appliances taken for granted elsewhere and until the 1960s it kept much of the labour force under the *mezzadria* system (sharecropping) as *contadini,* or peasants on small, inefficient farms whose wealthy owners paid them not in cash but in kind: half the crop. Depending on 'home-grown' thrift and caution, they developed a love for the land and its produce that is still strong. Italians still like to eat new peas in June and wild mushrooms in October, and open-air markets still thrive. They recognise such things as gifts from God and accord them almost religious veneration. In this chapter you will find recipes that offer a rich sampling of Italian vegetable specialities.

ZIA RITA'S
SMOTHERED CAULIFLOWER
Serves 4

Here is another of Zia Rita's inspired Italian recipes. The abundant quantity of delicious stock in this dish makes it imperative to serve the cauliflower with plenty of sturdy bread, which makes it a substantial side dish.

1 MEDIUM-SIZE HEAD CAULIFLOWER

4 GARLIC CLOVES, CRUSHED

4 TABLESPOONS EXTRA-VIRGIN OLIVE OIL

1 BUNCH SPRING ONIONS, TRIMMED AND THINLY SLICED, INCLUDING 50CM OF THE GREEN PART

SEA SALT TO TASTE

ZEST OF 1 LEMON

FRESHLY GROUND BLACK PEPPER

1 SMALL BUNCH FLAT-LEAF PARSLEY, CHOPPED

1. Trim only the tough leaves off the cauliflower, leaving any of the tender green ones intact. Cut the bottom so that it sits straight in the pan. Using a small knife, make a crisscross at the base of the head to allow the cooking heat to permeate the stem.

2. Select a deep pan just the right size to fit the cauliflower and high enough to fit a cover over it. The pan should be neither too large nor too tight-fitting. Warm the garlic in the oil in the pan over medium-low heat until it colours nicely, about 3 minutes. Add the cauliflower and strew one-third of the sliced spring onions, the salt, lemon zest and plenty of pepper over it. Add 250ml water. It should reach about halfway up the side of the cauliflower. Cover tightly and cook over medium heat for 5 minutes. Add the remaining spring onions and 3 tablespoons of the parsley. Add up to 250ml more of water if necessary to prevent the cauliflower from drying out. Simmer for 10 minutes, or until the water evaporates enough to form a rich, flavourful stock and the bottom of the cauliflower is tender when pierced with a skewer into the centre.

3. Bring the cauliflower to the table in a deep serving bowl in order to present it whole. Slice it at the table, cutting into wedges. Ladle some of the delicious stock over each portion and strew with the remaining parsley.

NONNA VERA'S
SWEET AND SOUR CARROTS

Serves 4

Vera Erenbourg D'Angara was a Russian painter and actress who was the first lady of the Russian theatre in Geneva at the turn of the last century. After the Russian revolution, she lost her fabulous wealth within three days and in 1918 was taken stateless and penniless to Rome by Anna Maria D'Annunzio. She was a gifted cook, and her granddaughter, my friend Anna Maria Erenbourg Weld, has kindly shared her recipes. Many, such as this lovely sweet-and-sour dish, are a combination of Russian and Italian cooking (also see Nonna Vera's Tender and Crunchy Beef Medallions, page 133).

10 CARROTS	50G SUGAR
4 TABLESPOONS EXTRA-VIRGIN OLIVE OIL	½ TEASPOON SALT
3 TABLESPOONS UNSALTED BUTTER	2 TABLESPOONS RED WINE VINEGAR
2 ONIONS, THINLY SLICED	

1. Peel the carrots and cut off their tops. Slice them into 5-mm rounds.

2. In a frying pan, warm the olive oil and butter together. Add the onions and carrots and 125ml water. Cover and allow the carrots to cook over medium heat until tender and the water is evaporated, stirring frequently, about 30 minutes. Sprinkle with the sugar, salt and vinegar. Continue to cook, uncovered, until the carrots and onions become caramelised, crisp at the edges and cast with a mahogany sheen. Serve at once.

SAUTÉED SWISS CHARD
WITH VINEGAR AND CRISPY BACON

Serves 4

Swiss chard and other greens are nourishing and good for the digestion. In southern Italy, they are a daily feature on the table. Lacinato (Tuscan) kale and spring greens can also be cooked this way. For a meatless version, omit the pancetta or bacon and substitute two or three additional tablespoons of olive oil.

350G SWISS CHARD	½ TEASPOON SEA SALT
2 TABLESPOONS EXTRA-VIRGIN OLIVE OIL	FRESHLY GROUND BLACK OR WHITE PEPPER
75G PANCETTA OR BACON, DICED	
4 LARGE SHALLOTS, FINELY CHOPPED	2 TABLESPOONS RED OR WHITE WINE VINEGAR, OR TO TASTE

1. Wash the chard well to dislodge any dirt clinging to the leaves. Drain any excess water but allow the water that clings to the leaves to remain. Use a sharp chef's knife to cut out the centre rib and stem of every leaf. The easiest way to do this is to fold the leaf in half lengthways and slice off the tough spine. Trim and discard the stems. Only if the stalks are tender, finely chop them. If they are tough, discard. Coarsely chop the greens.

2. In an ample nonreactive, non-stick casserole dish, warm the olive oil. Add the pancetta or bacon to the dish and sauté over medium heat until crisp and browned, 4 to 5 minutes. Use a slotted spoon to transfer to a side dish. Discard all but 4 tablespoons of fat from the pan.

3. Add the shallots and finely chopped stalks and sauté over medium-low heat until wilted, about 10 minutes. Add the greens to the dish and raise the heat to medium. Sauté, tossing occasionally, until the greens wilt completely but still retain their vivid colour, about 5 minutes. Season with salt and pepper, sprinkle with the vinegar and scatter with the pancetta or bacon. Serve hot.

TWO SIMPLE WAYS WITH
CABBAGE

Serve 6

In Italy, cabbage is cooked in many ways. The simplest is probably the Sardinian fashion of boiling cabbage in salted water until it is tender, and then sprinkling it with fruity olive oil (called *cauli a conca* in dialect). Even this elementary dish is delicious if the cabbage is young and fresh, and the oil full-bodied. It hardly seems necessary to write the method down for it. Another good, simple recipe is the way Anna Amendolara Nurse makes it, a version from Puglia. I especially like it with fennel seeds, but if serving it as an accompaniment with Moist Pan-Fried Pork Chops with Crunchy Crumb and Fennel Coating (page 126), substitute red pepper flakes.

2 TABLESPOONS EXTRA-VIRGIN OLIVE OIL

6 LARGE GARLIC CLOVES, SMASHED

75G PANCETTA, DICED

RED PEPPER FLAKES TO TASTE, OR
½ TEASPOON FENNEL SEEDS

1.1KG HEAD WHITE (STANDARD) CABBAGE,
CORED AND SHREDDED

1 TEASPOON SEA SALT, OR TO TASTE

1. In a cast-iron casserole dish with a heavy base, warm the olive oil. Stir in the garlic and sauté until lightly coloured, about 3 minutes. Remove the garlic and set aside.

2. Add the pancetta and the red pepper flakes or fennel seeds and sauté until golden, about 8 minutes. Stir in the cabbage and use a wooden spoon to toss well. Pour in 125ml water and cover. Steam until thoroughly tender, about 30 minutes; if the cabbage begins to dry out or stick to the base of the pan, add up to 60ml more water.

3. Return the garlic to the cabbage if you like, add the salt and serve.

WINTER SQUASH STEW
WITH TOMATO, DRY-CURED OLIVES AND GARLIC

Serves 6

The combination of fresh pumpkin, sour black dry-cured olives and tomatoes may sound unusual, but it is superb in this dish that I was raised on. Pumpkin or squash alone is bland, but the pungent dry-cured olives and garlic carry it to glory. Making this dish a day or two before you plan to serve it gives the flavours time to develop. Avoid serving it with other courses containing tomato sauce.

60ML EXTRA-VIRGIN OLIVE OIL

3 LARGE GARLIC CLOVES, SLICED

250ML TINNED PASSATA, OR 110G TOMATO PURÉE MIXED WITH 125ML WATER

1 MEDIUM-SIZE BUTTERNUT SQUASH OR 1 SMALL PUMPKIN (ABOUT 700G), PEELED, DESEEDED AND DICED

20 BLACK DRY-CURED MOROCCAN OLIVES, PITTED AND HALVED

1½ TEASPOONS CHOPPED FRESH THYME, OR ½ TEASPOON DRIED THYME

SEA SALT, TO TASTE

FRESHLY GROUND BLACK PEPPER

1. In a saucepan over medium heat, warm the oil and garlic together until the garlic is fragrant, about 4 minutes. Add the passata, stir and bring slowly to a simmer, about 4 minutes. Add the squash, olives, thyme and 175ml water. Cover partially and simmer gently until tender, about 40 minutes.

2. Season with salt and pepper to taste. Serve immediately or chill and reheat gently before serving.

AHEAD-OF-TIME NOTE: This dish can be made up to 3 days in advance.

CASA JANCA'S
ROASTED PEPPERS

Serves 4

Cookbook writer Rosetta Costantino, author of *My Calabria,* offered this recipe from Casa Janca, a rustic *agriturismo* near the fishing village of Pizzo in Calabria. The owner, Rita Callipo, is a highly regarded cook who runs a restaurant out of her home. The peppers can be served as a vegetable side dish or as an appetiser, as they do in Calabria.

60ML EXTRA-VIRGIN OLIVE OIL, PLUS MORE FOR GREASING

25G FRESHLY GRATED PECORINO CHEESE

25G OF FRESH BREADCRUMBS

1 LARGE GARLIC CLOVE, FINELY CHOPPED

2 TABLESPOONS FINELY CHOPPED FRESH FLAT-LEAF PARSLEY

4 MEDIUM-SIZE MIXED RED AND YELLOW BELL PEPPERS

SEA SALT

1 TABLESPOON CAPERS, CHOPPED IF USING LARGE CAPERS, OR CAPER BERRIES

6 ANCHOVY FILLETS, CUT IN SMALL PIECES

18 TO 20 SMALL CHERRY TOMATOES, CUT IN HALF OR QUARTERS IF LARGE

1. Preheat the oven to 200°C/400°F/gas mark 6. Lightly oil a baking tray large enough to fit the peppers once they are cut into eight halves. In a small bowl, combine the grated cheese, breadcrumbs, garlic and parsley and mix well.

2. Cut the peppers in half lengthways. Remove the stem and seeds. Place the peppers cut-side up in the baking tray. Sprinkle with a little salt, the capers or caper berries, anchovy pieces and cut-up tomatoes. Distribute the breadcrumb mixture on top and drizzle each pepper half with the olive oil.

3. Slide the peppers onto the middle rack of the oven; bake until the peppers are thoroughly soft and nicely coloured, about 45 minutes or longer, depending on the size of the peppers and their freshness.

4. Serve warm or at room temperature.

ANNA MARIA'S
ROASTED ONIONS WITH CRUMB TOPPING
Serves 4

Anna Maria Erenbourg Weld grew up in Rome watching her mother, grandmother and great-grandmother cook. The three generations of women shopped and cooked daily for their extended family, which included eight relatives and the maid. Their cooking combined the traditions of both the Rome and Romagna branches of the matriarchy. This is one of their delicious vegetable dishes, suitable as a side dish or an appetiser.

6 TABLESPOONS EXTRA-VIRGIN OLIVE OIL

8 SWEET, YELLOW ONIONS (ABOUT 700G)

6 TABLESPOONS BREADCRUMBS

1 TABLESPOON FINELY CHOPPED FRESH FLAT-LEAF PARSLEY

½ TEASPOON SEA SALT

FRESHLY GROUND BLACK PEPPER

1. Preheat the oven to 230°C/450°F/gas mark 8. Grease 2 baking trays well with the 6 tablespoons extra-virgin olive oil.

2. Peel the onions and cut them into horizontal slices 5mm thick. Transfer the slices to the baking trays and slide them in the olive oil on both sides to coat evenly and distribute the oil evenly in the tray at the same time.

3. In a small bowl, combine the breadcrumbs, parsley, salt and pepper to taste. Sprinkle the breadcrumb mixture evenly over each of the onion slices. Distribute a total of 12 tablespoons water around the slices in both baking trays. Slide onto the middle and upper racks of the oven and bake until the onions are tender and almost transparent within and browned and crunchy on the surface, about 20 minutes. Serve hot or at room temperature, as preferred.

CREAMY MASHED POTATOES
WITH GARLIC

Serves 4

In the Italian fashion of making mashed potatoes, the cooked potatoes are mashed, then returned to the pan and whipped slowly as butter, followed by hot milk, are beaten into them until they are creamy, light and fluffy. These puréed potatoes are indispensable with many of the meat dishes in this book. You can include the garlic or not. In this version, abundant garlic is boiled with the potatoes until it is soft and creamy, and the lot is later mashed together.

700G MATURE BOILING POTATOES OR YUKON GOLD POTATOES

12 LARGE GARLIC CLOVES, SKINS ON

4 TABLESPOONS UNSALTED BUTTER, CUT INTO THIN SLICES

SEA SALT

175ML HOT MILK

FRESHLY GROUND WHITE PEPPER

1. Reject any potatoes that are green, or cut off any green parts. Scrub the potatoes well but leave their skins on.

2. Place the potatoes in a saucepan with enough cold water to cover. Partially cover the pot and bring to a boil over high heat. Reduce the heat to medium and continue to cook until the potatoes are tender, about 30 minutes. Drop the garlic cloves in the water 15 minutes before the potatoes are done. Test for doneness by inserting a cake tester or a sharp knife into the potatoes and garlic.

3. Drain the potatoes and garlic and allow them to cool just until they are comfortable to handle. Rinse the pot. Peel the potatoes and the garlic and pass them through a potato ricer back into the pot. (In a potato ricer, the potatoes are forced through small holes, with the result that there will be no lumps in the mashed potatoes.) If a potato ricer is not available, transfer the peeled potatoes and garlic to the pot and use a potato masher to thoroughly mash them and press out any lumps.

4. Place the pot over the lowest possible heat and stir constantly as you work to prevent the potatoes on the bottom of the pan from becoming scorched. Add the butter, and salt to taste. Use an electric beater if available, or a whisk, to beat the potatoes while pouring in the hot milk a little at a time. The potatoes will become light and creamy.

5. Remove the pot from the heat. Adjust for salt and add pepper to taste, beating with the beater or whisk. Serve immediately.

ZIA RITA'S
POTATOES SCHISCIONERA
Serves 6

Another of my aunt's infallible Sardinian recipes, these potatoes are stewed slowly with garlic, celery heart and parsley, which makes them creamy and flavourful. This is a lovely side dish with Whole Roasted Chicken with Garlic, Fresh Garden Herbs and Gravy (page 112), Luisa Petruccci's Oven-Fried Chicken with Breadcrumbs (page 120), Nonna Vera's Tender and Crunchy Beef Medallions (page 133), or Juicy Meat Loaf with Tomato and Red Wine Glaze (page 136).

2 TABLESPOONS EXTRA-VIRGIN OLIVE OIL, PLUS MORE FOR FINISHING

2 LARGE GARLIC CLOVES, FINELY CHOPPED OR GRATED

5 MEDIUM-SIZE BOILING POTATOES (ABOUT 700G), PEELED AND CUT INTO 2.5-CM CUBES

SEA SALT TO TASTE

FRESHLY GROUND BLACK PEPPER

3 CELERY STICKS FROM THE HEART, PLUS TENDER LEAVES, CHOPPED

4 TABLESPOONS CHOPPED FRESH FLAT-LEAF PARSLEY

Place the oil and garlic in a cold saucepan large enough to accommodate the potatoes later. Turn on the heat to low and sauté until the garlic is softened, about 2 minutes. Add the potatoes and stir. Add 250ml water, the salt, pepper to taste, the celery heart and half the parsley. Cover and simmer over medium heat until the potatoes are tender, about 20 minutes, stirring occasionally as they cook to prevent them from sticking to the pan. Stir in the remaining parsley and celery leaves. Drizzle with a little more olive oil to taste. Serve.

AHEAD-OF-TIME NOTE: This dish can be made up to 2 days in advance, then cooled, covered and refrigerated. Reheat gently over low heat.

VIOLA BUITONI'S
SAUTÉED BROCCOLI RAPINI WITH POTATOES

Serves 4

America has at last discovered this wonderful vegetable (often called 'raab' in English), but I'm convinced that people would like it more if they had it prepared correctly. The secret to cooking broccoli *rapini* is to boil the greens briefly before sautéing, to rid them of their excessive bitterness and to tenderise the stalks.

2 YUKON GOLD POTATOES, UNPEELED

1 BUNCH BROCCOLI RABE, ABOUT 700G

1 TABLESPOON SEA SALT

5 TABLESPOONS EXTRA-VIRGIN OLIVE OIL

6 LARGE GARLIC CLOVES, BRUISED BUT LEFT WHOLE

1. In a saucepan, combine the potatoes with enough cold water to cover and bring to the boil. Cook over medium heat until the potatoes are tender, about 20 minutes. They should be fully tender but not falling apart when cooked. When cool enough to handle, peel the skin from the potatoes, cut them lengthways into quarters and then cut crossways into medium-thin slices. Set aside.

2. Using a small, sharp knife, peel the skin from the tough lower stalks of the *rapini* (most of the bottom portion of the stalk) and cut them crossways into 7.5-cm lengths. Fill a large pot with plenty of water to cover the greens and bring to a rolling boil. Add the greens along with the salt, cover partially and cook until the stalks are completely tender but not mushy, about 5 minutes after the water returns to the boil. Note that if the stalks are at all crisp, they will remain bitter. Drain the greens, reserving a little of the cooking liquid. Set aside separately.

3. In a non-stick frying pan large enough to accommodate the potatoes and the greens, warm 3 tablespoons of the olive oil and add the garlic. Sauté over medium heat until the garlic is nicely softened but not coloured, about 4 minutes. Transfer to a bowl. Raise the heat to medium-high and add the potatoes. Sauté until they are golden and crispy all over, about 12 minutes, then transfer to another bowl. Warm the remaining 2 tablespoons olive oil over medium heat, then return the *rapini* and the garlic cloves to the pan. Sauté until the greens are nicely coated with the olive oil and the garlic and heated through, about 3 minutes; if they appear a little dry, add a little of the reserved cooking water as needed. Return the potatoes to the pan and toss all together. Adjust for seasoning and serve immediately.

CHAPTER

10

SUNDAY TREATS:
FRUIT DESSERTS, SWEETS
AND CONFECTIONS

Innumerable *pasticcerie,* or pastry shops, offer the fine and fancy year-round while home cooks produce uncomplicated, homespun desserts that often – like so much else in the Italian kitchen—appear according to season or occasion (engagements, weddings, religious feasts or festivals). Sweet yeast breads enriched with almonds or candied fruit are typical, and there are countless sugar-dusted fritters along the lines of *zeppole,* and of course *biscotti* (which means, literally, 'twice cooked'). There are specialities that are only made on particular religious holidays or festivities, or that are traditional for engagements, *carnevale,* or other significant occasions. The 'love knots' recipe in this chapter is my grandmother's. My father craved these Pugliese cookies, which his sister baked for him every year on his birthday until he died at the age of 100. Such desserts are as versatile as they are uncomplicated and homespun. Italians serve them at breakfast, as snacks and after dinner.

ANNA AMENDOLARA'S
BAKED APPLES WITH GRENADINE
Serves 4

Another of my friend Anna Amendolara's comforting home recipes, these baked apples are delicious with cream or vanilla ice cream. Grenadine, the prominent flavouring, is pomegranate syrup. You can find it in your supermarket, usually in the section where cocktail mixes are sold.

4 LARGE COOKING APPLES, PREFERABLY BRAMLEYS

4 TEASPOONS CASTER SUGAR

1 TEASPOON CINNAMON

175ML GRENADINE SYRUP

DOUBLE CREAM OR VANILLA ICE CREAM, TO SERVE

1. Preheat the oven to 190°C/375°F/gas mark 5.

2. Remove the stems and cut out the blossom ends of the apples. Do not core through but peel one-third down from the top. Place in a baking tin large enough to accommodate all the apples without touching. Sprinkle with the sugar and cinnamon. Pour grenadine over each apple. Add 150ml water to the tin and bake, uncovered, until soft, 45 minutes.

3. Serve warm or cold, with cream or vanilla ice cream.

ORANGE-ALMOND RING CAKE
WITH ORANGE GLAZE

Serves 8 to 10

I learned this lovely recipe from my friend, baker and food writer Susan G. Purdy, who discovered this moist cake bursting with citrus flavour in a seaside restaurant in Liguria. It has a slightly crunchy texture due to the ground almonds, but the predominant flavour is orange, enhanced by flecks of bright zest and an orange glaze. If you prefer a stronger almond flavour, you can substitute almond extract for the orange or use half almond and half orange.

SOLID VEGETABLE FAT OR UNSALTED BUTTER, FOR GREASING

155G SIFTED PLAIN FLOUR, PLUS EXTRA FOR DUSTING

175G WHOLE OR FLAKED ALMONDS (BLANCHED OR WITH SKINS)

300G GRANULATED SUGAR

2½ TEASPOONS BAKING POWDER

¾ TEASPOON SEA SALT

3 LARGE EGGS, SEPARATED, PLUS 2 WHOLE LARGE EGGS, AT ROOM TEMPERATURE

¼ TEASPOON CREAM OF TARTAR

125ML GRAPESEED OIL OR VEGETABLE OIL

4 TEASPOONS GRATED ORANGE ZEST

1 TABLESPOON EXTRA-FINE JULIENNED ORANGE ZEST (FROM 2 LARGE NAVEL ORANGES)

1¾ TEASPOONS PURE ORANGE EXTRACT

175ML FRESHLY SQUEEZED ORANGE JUICE WITH PULP, AT ROOM TEMPERATURE

FOR THE GLAZE

180G SIFTED ICING SUGAR

1 TABLESPOON GRATED ORANGE ZEST, PLUS THE JUICE OF 1 ORANGE AT ROOM TEMPERATURE

1 TEASPOON FRESHLY SQUEEZED LEMON JUICE, AT ROOM TEMPERATURE

EQUIPMENT

24-CM BUNDT TIN OR RING MOULD

1. Preheat the oven to 180°C/350°F/gas mark 4. Generously coat the inside of the bundt tin or ring mould with the vegetable fat or butter, then dust with flour; tap out excess flour.

2. In a food-processor fitted with a steel blade, combine the almonds with 50g of the granulated sugar. Pulse until the almonds are finely ground, 1 to 2 minutes, then turn them out into a bowl. In another bowl, whisk together the flour, baking powder and salt, then whisk into the almonds.

3. In the large bowl of an electric mixer, combine 3 egg whites and the cream of tartar; reserve the yolks in a separate bowl. Whip until the whites are foamy, then continue to whip on medium speed while slowly adding 150g the sugar. Whip until soft peaks form, then transfer to a clean bowl.

4. In the previously used mixer bowl, combine the reserved yolks plus 2 extra

whole eggs, the oil, the remaining 100g of the sugar, both the grated and julienned orange zest and the orange extract. Beat on high for about 2 minutes, until pale in colour. With the mixer on low speed, add the orange juice and beat for another minute. Remove the bowl from the mixer stand. By hand, fold in the flour-almond mix, then the egg whites, in three separate additions, to lighten the mixture.

5. Scoop the mixture into the prepared pan, smooth the top, and bake on the middle rack of the oven for 35 to 40 minutes, or until a cake tester inserted in the centre comes out clean. Cool the cake in its tin on a wire rack for at least 20 minutes. Invert the cake onto a rack or plate and cool completely.

6. While the cake is cooling, prepare the glaze. In a bowl, whisk together the icing sugar, the orange juice and the lemon juice until smooth and slightly runny. Drizzle the glaze over the cooled cake and sprinkle the grated orange zest over the top.

SUNDAY TREATS: FRUIT DESSERTS, SWEETS AND CONFECTIONS

NONNA CLIA'S
APPLE CAKE
Serves 6

The recipe for this typical Italian cake is kindly offered by my friend Flavia Destefanis. She writes, 'My maternal grandmother, Clia, who loved her country house in Montepulciano, near Siena, would whip this up for an afternoon tea. Egg size always depended on the whim of the chicken in our chicken coop. Quantities were never set in stone, nor were the ingredients: sometimes she added the zest of a lemon and no vanilla, sometimes she would throw in a few walnuts if she had the inkling. Any flaws that might show up were covered up by the dusting of sugar.' This cake can be made with other types of fruit that are in season, such as plums, washed, dried and quartered, or apricots, or a combination of apples and pears. Just add a bit more flour if the fruit is quite wet.

SOLID VEGETABLE FAT OR BUTTER, FOR GREASING

3 LARGE EGGS

5 TABLESPOONS GRANULATED SUGAR

1 TEASPOON PURE VANILLA EXTRACT

10 TABLESPOONS UNSALTED BUTTER, MELTED AND COOLED

155G PLAIN UNBLEACHED FLOUR, PLUS EXTRA FOR DUSTING

1 TEASPOON BAKING POWDER

1 TEASPOON BICARBONATE OF SODA

⅛ TEASPOON SALT

4 MEDIUM-SIZE APPLES, PEELED, CORED, AND CUT INTO 2-CM CUBES

ICING SUGAR, FOR DUSTING

EQUIPMENT

23-CM SPRINGFORM CAKE TIN, PREFERABLY, BUT ANY TIN WILL DO

1. Preheat the oven to 190°C/375°F/gas mark 5. Select a 23-cm springform cake tin with sides that are at least 5cm high. Generously grease the tin with solid vegetable fat or butter and dust with flour. Tap out the excess flour and set aside.

2. In a mixing bowl, beat the eggs. Whisk in the granulated sugar and vanilla until blended, about 45 seconds. Stir in the butter. Sift in the flour, baking powder, bicarbonate of soda and salt until just combined to form a thick, sticky mixture. Additional flour may be necessary, depending on the size of the eggs. Fold in the apple cubes and transfer the batter to the prepared pan.

3. Bake until golden brown and a cake tester inserted into the centre comes out clean, 35 to 40 minutes. Cool on a wire rack for at least 20 minutes, then run a paring knife around the sides of the tin to loosen. Place a wire rack over the tin and invert the tin and wire rack together. Lift off the cake tin and let the cake cool right-side up for 20 minutes, then transfer to a serving platter. Dust the surface with icing sugar. Cut into wedges, and serve.

AUNT NETTIE'S
ITALIAN CHEESECAKE
Serves 8 to 10

My aunt and godmother, Annette Messina, was a superb baker and she was famous for this ricotta cheesecake. The base is a classic *pasta frolla*, a sweet, biscuit-like dough. As with most cheesecakes, this tart must be aged to develop its flavour. It should be made at least a day in advance, and is best eaten within 2 or 3 days, but it will keep for up to 1 week, chilled.

FOR THE BASE:

250G SIFTED UNBLEACHED PLAIN FLOUR

110G GRANULATED SUGAR

PINCH OF SALT

8 TABLESPOONS COLD UNSALTED BUTTER, PLUS EXTRA FOR GREASING

1 LARGE EGG, BEATEN WITH 1 TABLESPOON MILK

FOR THE FILLING

625G DRAINED FRESH WHOLE-MILK RICOTTA

4 EXTRA-LARGE EGGS

190G GRANULATED SUGAR

40G PLAIN UNBLEACHED FLOUR

225G FULL-FAT CREAM CHEESE, AT ROOM TEMPERATURE

GRATED ZEST OF 1 ORANGE

GRATED ZEST OF 1 LEMON

½ TEASPOON GROUND CINNAMON

60ML RUM

20G CHOPPED CANDIED ORANGE PEEL

45G CHOPPED DARK CHOCOLATE (70% COCOA SOLIDS)

120G DOUBLE CREAM

1CING SUGAR, FOR DUSTING

EQUIPMENT

20-CM SPRINGFORM CAKE TIN

1. First make the crust: sift the flour, granulated sugar and salt together into a medium bowl. Using 2 dinner knives, cut in the butter until a crumb-like mixture is formed. Using a fork, mix the beaten egg into the flour mixture until evenly moistened. Using your hands, gather the dough into a ball. Wrap the ball in clingfilm and refrigerate for 1 hour or overnight before using.

2. Generously butter the cake tin. Preheat the oven to 180°C/350°F/gas mark 4. Sprinkle a work surface lightly with flour and roll the ball of dough into a disc 2.5mm thick. Crimp aluminium foil under and around the sides of the tin to catch any leaks during baking. Fit the dough into the tin and crimp the edges. Refrigerate the dough-lined tin until ready for use.

3. To make the filling, place the ricotta into a strainer and set it over a bowl; press out the excess liquid. Beat the eggs well, then brush some of the beaten egg into the dough-lined tin to moisture-proof it. Add 190g sugar and the flour to the remaining eggs and beat for 2 to 3 minutes, until thick and a light yellow color.

Add the drained ricotta and cream cheese and beat until smooth. Add the zests, cinnamon and rum and beat until smooth. Stir in about half of the orange peel and chocolate. Sprinkle the other half over the glazed dough-lined tin.

5. In a deep bowl, beat the double cream with the 2 tablespoons sugar until soft peaks form. Fold into the ricotta mixture until blended. Pour the ricotta filling into the prepared tin and smooth the top evenly. Slide the tin onto the middle rack of the oven and bake for 1 hour and 15 minutes. Turn off the oven and leave the cake inside with the door closed for about 1 hour. Take out and cool completely. Remove the sides of the springform tin. Slide the cake onto a cake platter, cover with clingfilm, and refrigerate overnight before serving.

6. Before serving, dust the cheesecake with icing sugar. The cheesecake is usually cut into small slices and accompanied with espresso.

AUNT NETTIE'S
SWEET LOVE KNOTS
Makes 8 to 9 dozen

The recipe for this traditional biscuit, *taralli dolci*, of the Puglia region came from my paternal grandmother but my aunt, a talented baker, fiddled with the original recipe whenever she made it until her *taralli* were the best and the lightest I've ever had. This is how she does it.

500G UNSIFTED PLAIN FLOUR, PLUS EXTRA

340G GRANULATED SUGAR (300G IF YOU LIKE IT LESS SWEET)

6 TEASPOONS BAKING POWDER

16 TABLESPOONS UNSALTED BUTTER, AT ROOM TEMPERATURE

8 EXTRA-LARGE EGGS

3 TABLESPOONS PURE VANILLA EXTRACT

FOR THE GLAZE

180G ICING SUGAR

125ML WATER OR MILK

1. Preheat the oven to 180°C/350°F/gas mark 4.

2. In a mixing bowl, combine the flour, granulated sugar and baking powder. Cut the butter into the flour mixture as if making pastry. If mixing by hand, make a 'well' in the centre of the mixture.

3. Beat the eggs with the vanilla and pour them into the well. Gradually add the flour into the eggs until it is all incorporated. Wash hands well and mix and knead the dough until smooth. You may have to add more flour until the dough is soft but workable. Turn the dough out onto a clean, lightly floured work surface. Keep adding a little flour to the surface, as necessary, as you are shaping the dough if it sticks.

4. To form the biscuits, take a piece of dough the size of a walnut and roll it with your hands on the work surface to form a log about the size of your middle finger. Then take one end of the log and place it over the opposite end so that a small hole remains in the centre. Place the 'love knots' on baking trays about 2.5cm apart. Bake until lightly browned, about 18 minutes.

5. While the biscuits are baking, make the glaze. In a medium bowl, whisk the icing sugar with the water until smooth. While the biscuits are cooling, brush the tops with the glaze; it should have a thick consistency, as it will melt on the surface and form a thick glaze as the *taralli* cool.

SWEET EASTER BREAD

Makes 2 loaves

This delicious, delicate sweet bread is traditional in many Italian homes on Easter morning with boiled eggs to symbolise rebirth, along with a platter of *salumi*. The sweet bread resembles panettone, but is less buttery. One of the many variations of this bread relies on cinnamon for flavouring, which may be included here if you like. Others include the addition of sultanas or diced candied fruit. The recipe should be started early in the day, as some five or six hours are necessary for it to rise. It is better to use a heavy-duty electric mixer than to work by hand, as the dough requires extensive kneading before the first rise.

FOR THE SPONGE

125ML WARM MILK (40 TO 46°C) OR LUKEWARM MILK (27 TO 32°C)

3½ TEASPOONS EASY BLEND YEAST OR 1½ CAKES COMPRESSED YEAST

70G BREAD FLOUR

FOR THE DOUGH

SPONGE, AS ABOVE

10 EXTRA-LARGE EGG YOLKS AT ROOM TEMPERATURE

150G GRANULATED SUGAR

9 TABLESPOONS UNSALTED BUTTER, AT ROOM TEMP, PLUS EXTRA FOR GREASING

125ML MILK

GRATED ZEST OF 4 LEMONS

2 TEASPOONS PURE VANILLA EXTRACT

2 TABLESPOONS ROSE WATER

2 TEASPOONS GROUND CINNAMON (OPTIONAL)

470G BREAD FLOUR

1 EXTRA-LARGE EGG WHITE, LIGHTLY BEATEN

ICING SUGAR, FOR DUSTING

1. In the bowl of an electric mixer, stir the warm milk and dry yeast together until dissolved. Leave until foamy, about 12 minutes. Stir in the flour. Cover tightly with clingfilm and rest until doubled in size and spongy in texture, about 1 hour.

2. To make the dough, fit the mixer with the paddle attachment and attach the bowl with the sponge. With the machine running, add the egg yolks, one at a time. Add the granulated sugar and beat until creamy, then gradually add the butter, milk, lemon zest, vanilla, rose water, cinnamon (if using) and flour. Beat on medium for at least 12 minutes, stopping occasionally to scrape down the sides, until the dough is barely sticky. Cover tightly with clingfilm wrap, then with a clean tea towel. Leave to rise in a warm, draft-free place until tripled in size, about 3 hours.

3. Generously butter 2 loaf tins. Knock back the dough and turn it out onto a floured work surface. Grease your hands with butter or olive oil and knead the dough to work out the large bubbles, about 5 minutes. It should remain very soft, almost

sticky, and elastic. Divide the dough in half and place each half in one of the buttered loaf tins. Cover the tins tightly with clingfilm and cover with tea towels. Leave to rise once again until the dough doubles in size, about 2½ hours.

4. Preheat the oven to 190°C/375°F/gas mark 5. Brush the surface of each loaf with the egg white and slide the tins onto the middle rack of the oven. Bake until golden, about 12 minutes. Cover loosely with aluminium foil and bake about 20 minutes longer, until the top of the loaves balloon into a great dome and are golden brown. Remove and leave to cool for about 5 minutes, then carefully transfer to wire racks to cool. When the loaves are completely cool, dust generously with icing sugar.

NONNA MESSINA'S
ITALIAN SESAME SEED COOKIES

Makes 8 Dozen

My aunt learned to make many Sicilian sweets from her Sicilian mother-in-law, Santa Messina, a widow who devoted her life to cooking and baking for her sons. These classic biscuits, while simple, turned up at festivities, but they are terrific at breakfast for dunking into espresso or coffee. They will keep for up to 3 months or more in a closed container placed in a cool, dry place. If using a food-processor, you will need to halve the recipe.

400G UNBLEACHED PLAIN FLOUR	2 LARGE EGGS, LIGHTLY BEATEN
340G SUGAR	125ML MILK, PLUS 60ML FOR BRUSHING
1 TABLESPOON BAKING POWDER	1 TEASPOON PURE VANILLA EXTRACT
½ TEASPOON SALT	260G UNSALTED SESAME SEEDS
6 TABLESPOONS UNSALTED BUTTER	(TOASTED OR UNTOASTED)

1. Sift the dry ingredients into a mixing bowl. Cut in the butter with two knives until it resembles coarse crumbs.

2. Combine the eggs, milk and vanilla and stir them into the dry ingredients to make a soft dough. Chill the dough for 1 hour.

3. Preheat the oven to 190°C/375°F/gas mark 5. Line two baking trays with greaseproof paper.

4. Form the dough into 'ropes' about 6.5cm long and 1cm in diameter. Brush the pieces with milk and roll them in the sesame seeds until they are well covered. Place 2.5cm apart on the baking trays and bake for 20 to 25 minutes, or until golden. Remove from the oven and transfer to racks to cool.

FRAPPE

These addictive Italian pastry fritters are inescapable in the repertoire of Italian sweets, and there are many names for them. My mother called them *frappe* and my paternal grandmother called them *cartedatte*. My mother's were lighter, but my grandmother Domenica made a beautiful syrup for dunking or pouring over them (see opposite). The best pastries of this genre are very crisp and so delicately thin that they are in essence *vaporoso*, 'like vapour', as the Italians sometimes say. It is better if the dough incorporates grappa, wine or some kind of liquor, as it causes the pastries to fry up crisp and makes them light. Another rule is to roll out the dough as thin as possible. I always use a hand-cranked pasta machine, passing the dough through the rollers set on the last notch. *Frappe* can be eaten right after they are cooked, or up to a couple of weeks afterwards if stored in tightly sealed tins at room temperature to ensure their crispness.

GENEROUS 200G UNBLEACHED PLAIN FLOUR, OR AS NEEDED

2 TABLESPOONS COLD UNSALTED BUTTER, CUT INTO SMALL PIECES

3 EXTRA-LARGE EGGS AT ROOM TEMPERATURE

3 TABLESPOONS GRANULATED SUGAR

¼ TEASPOON SALT

60ML DRY VERMOUTH, DRY SHERRY, GRAPPA, OR RUM

CORN OIL, FOR DEEP-FRYING

ICING SUGAR, FOR DUSTING

1. To make by hand, sift the flour into a bowl. Add the butter pieces and, using your fingers or a pastry blender, work them in until the mixture is the consistency of coarse crumbs. Turn the mixture out onto a work surface. Using your fingers, make a well in the centre of the mound.

2. In a bowl, stir together the eggs, granulated sugar, salt and wine or grappa with a fork until blended. Pour the mixture into the well and, using the fork and always stirring in the same direction, draw the dry ingredients into the wet ingredients. When a pliable dough begins to form, set the fork aside and work with your hands. If too soft, sprinkle in flour a little at a time – but the dough shouldn't be too stiff.

3. To make in a food processor, put the flour and butter into the bowl and process until the butter becomes crumb-like, about 30 seconds. Add the eggs, granulated sugar, salt and wine or grappa and process until a smooth dough forms.

4. Divide the dough into 4 equal portions. Work with 1 portion at a time, keeping the other portions covered with a clean, slightly damp tea towel. On a floured work surface, use a rolling pin to roll out the dough paper-thin – the thinner, the better.

Alternatively, divide the dough into 8 equal portions, and roll out each portion into the thinnest strip possible on a hand-cranked pasta machine: start out at the widest setting and pass the dough through each consecutive setting once, ending with the last setting. If the dough sticks, dust it lightly with flour before passing it through the rollers.

5. Cut the dough strip into rectangles about 5 x 7.5cm. Make a horizontal cut in the centre of each rectangle; this helps them fry evenly. Spread the rectangles out on clean, dry tea towels. Cover them with more clean, dry tea towels. Roll out and cut the remaining dough portions in the same way.

6. Pour the corn oil into a deep frying pan to a depth of 5cm and heat over high heat until a scrap of dough sizzles upon contact. Add the dough rectangles, a few at a time, but do not crowd the pan. There should be enough oil around each rectangle to allow quick and even cooking. Fry, turning once, until evenly golden on both sides, about 2 minutes. Adjust the heat if the pastries are browning too quickly. Using a wire skimmer, transfer to kitchen paper to drain. You can stack them, but put kitchen paper between the layers to absorb the excess oil. When all of the pastries are fried, leave to cool completely, then dust generously with icing sugar.

NONNA DOMENICA'S
RAISIN SAUCE WITH PORT WINE

Makes 880ml

The aroma of fruit, port and cinnamon always reminds me of Christmas. The original recipe called for *vin santo*, which is difficult to find outside Italy, but I find that port wine works splendidly. Serve alongside rice or bread puddings, or with the *frappe* as a dipping sauce.

450G RAISINS	PINCH OF FRESHLY GRATED NUTMEG
250ML PORT WINE	1 CINNAMON STICK
½ TEASPOON CLOVES	170G HONEY

1. In a medium saucepan, bring the raisins in 750ml of water to a boil. Cover the pan, lower the heat to a simmer, and cook for 1 hour. Strain the raisins through a food mill. You should have approximately 500ml of syrup.

2. Return the syrup to the pan and add the port, cloves, nutmeg, cinnamon and honey. Simmer for another 30 minutes. Leave to cool before using.

VENETIAN PUDDING
WITH CUSTARD SAUCE

Serves 6 to 8

I adapted this recipe for fragrant bread pudding from an old Venetian dessert designed for using up stale bread. It is light and delicate due in part to the fact that the 'stale' bread is finely shredded before it soaks in the milk. Ginger, orange zest, cinnamon and mace enhance it with their beguiling flavours and scents. I like to serve custard with it, but offer it with whipped cream instead, if you prefer. Note: the easiest way to grate fresh ginger is to peel it when it is fresh and freeze it until ready to use; it grates very easily when it is frozen solid.

450G CRUST-FREE, STALE CHALLAH-STYLE BREAD (ABOUT 600G WITH CRUST)

1 LITRE MILK

50G ALMONDS, GROUND

50G WALNUTS, GROUND

100G SULTANAS

1 TABLESPOON FRESHLY GRATED ZEST OF 1 LARGE NAVEL ORANGE

1 TABLESPOON GRATED FRESH GINGER

7 TABLESPOONS CASTER SUGAR

2 TABLESPOONS HONEY

½ TEASPOON GROUND MACE

1 TEASPOON GROUND CINNAMON

¼ TEASPOON SEA SALT

5 EXTRA-LARGE EGGS, SEPARATED

UNSALTED BUTTER, FOR GREASING

10G FINE, FRESH WHITE BREADCRUMBS, FOR COATING

FOR THE CUSTARD

5 TEASPOONS CASTER SUGAR

1 EGG YOLK

1 HEAPED TABLESPOON CORNFLOUR

250ML MILK

SMALL PINCH OF SALT

2.5-CM STRIP OF LEMON ZEST

1. Preheat the oven to 190°C/375°F/gas mark 5.

2. Using your fingers, tear the bread into thin shreds. In a large bowl, combine the shredded bread and the milk and leave to soak for 10 to 15 minutes. Toss occasionally to ensure even soaking. Mix in the ground nuts, sultanas, orange zest, ginger, sugar, honey, mace, cinnamon and salt.

3. In a separate bowl, beat the egg yolks until light yellow and blended. Add to the bread mixture and blend. In yet another bowl, using an electric mixer, beat the egg whites until they begin to form peaks easily, but are not so stiff that they begin to separate into liquid and solid parts. Using a large rubber or plastic spatula, gently fold the whites into the bread mixture just until no white streaks remain.

4. Select a wide, shallow baking tin about 23 x 33 x 5cm. If it is too deep, the pudding will be too moist in the centre. Grease the tin generously with butter.

Sprinkle the breadcrumbs into the tin evenly, then tilt the tin to coat the entire surface with a uniform layer. Tap out any excess. Pour the filling into the prepared baking tin, taking care not to disturb the coating on the tin and smoothing the surface to ensure an equal depth throughout. Bake until nicely golden brown, about 40 minutes. Turn off the oven and leave the pudding to rest in the oven for another 10 to 15 minutes. Remove the tin from the oven and leave the pudding to cool completely on a rack.

5. While the bread pudding is cooling, make the custard. In a saucepan, add the sugar to the egg yolk and beat with a whisk for a few minutes until creamy. Add the cornflour, beating to incorporate. Add 2 tablespoons of the milk, using a wooden spoon to make a creamy mixture. Add the salt and lemon zest to the rest of the milk. Place the pan over low heat and gradually add the rest of the milk mixture. Stir constantly until the mixture begins to simmer gently and thickens enough to coat a spoon. Remove from the hob, cover and keep warm.

6. Cut the bread pudding into squares or rectangles, as desired. Place a tablespoon or two of the warm custard on individual serving plates. Lay a portion of the pudding over the custard and serve.

11

BABY'S FIRST FOOD
(GROWN-UPS LOVE IT TOO)

Italians eat well as adults because they ate well as children. They grew up on wholesome food, the food their elders ate, not baby food or toddler's food or sugar-, fat- or salt-laden stuff made in factories, processed with chemicals for long, perhaps eternal shelf-life and enhanced profit margins. Italian parents are attentive to nutritious, natural food, made always from the freshest and finest ingredients, and not only in their homes. It is not unusual to see an Italian youngster in a restaurant, being tutored on the fine points of good eating by his parents and even by the waiters. There are recipes in this chapter for comforting foods Italian children grow up with. I chose them because they are quick to prepare and are nourishing, but they are no less appealing to adults.

ALPHABET AND VEGETABLE SOUP
WITH MOZZARELLA DICE

Serves 4 children

Children have fun fishing for pasta alphabets in their soup and then eating them. When I was a child in the 1950s, the closest my American schoolmates got to this traditional childhood classic was tinned alphabet soup – and they loved it. The nutritious homemade version (the corn is a recent addition) is better, I promise – and you won't have any trouble getting little ones to eat it. If you like, drop in diced mozzarella or 'string cheese' before serving, as my mother often did; children love the oozy strings of cheese as it melts in the hot stock.

1 FRESH EAR OF CORN

1 LEAF SWISS CHARD

1 LITRE VEGETABLE STOCK (PAGE 215) OR CHICKEN STOCK (PAGE 214)

1 SMALL CELERY STICK, INCLUDING LEAVES, STRINGS REMOVED, FINELY DICED

1 SMALL CARROT, FINELY DICED

1 FRESH OR TINNED PLUM TOMATO, PEELED, DESEEDED AND CHOPPED

1 SMALL COURGETTE, FINELY DICED

1 SMALL ONION OR 1 SHALLOT, FINELY DICED

1 TEASPOON SEA SALT, OR TO TASTE

40G ALPHABET PASTINA

30G MOZZARELLA OR 'STRING CHEESE', FINELY DICED (OPTIONAL)

1. Slice the kernels off the ear of corn. Cut the thick rib off the chard and finely chop it. Chop the leafy part and set all aside.

2. Pour the stock into a saucepan and stir in the celery, chard, carrot, and tomato. Simmer, partially covered, until they are tender, about 20 minutes. Add the corn, courgette, onion or shallot, salt and alphabet pastina and simmer for another 5 minutes, or less, until the pastina is cooked to your liking. If adding the cheese, drop it into each individual bowl. Serve.

SEMOLINA
IN STOCK

Serves 4 children or 3 adults

This is a smooth, comforting soup that children love. You can buy coarsely ground semolina, which resembles polenta meal, in health food stores and some Italian speciality shops.

2 TABLESPOONS EXTRA-VIRGIN OLIVE OIL OR UNSALTED BUTTER

6 SPRING ONIONS, FINELY CHOPPED

2 SWEET PLUM TOMATOES, PEELED, DESEEDED AND CHOPPED

2 TABLESPOONS FINELY CHOPPED FRESH FLAT-LEAF PARSLEY

950ML CHICKEN STOCK (PAGE 214)

40G COARSE SEMOLINA

SEA SALT AND FRESHLY GROUND BLACK OR WHITE PEPPER

FRESHLY GRATED PARMIGIANO-REGGIANO OR GRANA PADANO CHEESE, TO SERVE

1. Warm the olive oil or butter in a medium saucepan. Stir in the spring onions and sauté to wilt, about 1 minute. Add the tomatoes and parsley and sauté for an additional minute. Stir in the stock and bring it to the boil. Immediately reduce to a simmer over medium-low heat and whisk in the semolina. Lower the heat to medium-low and simmer, stirring, until the semolina absorbs the liquid thoroughly and the soup coats a wooden spoon – it should be neither too thick nor too thin – about 7 minutes. Take care not to allow the soup to get too dense. Taste and season with salt and pepper.

2. Ladle the soup into serving bowls and sprinkle grated cheese over each portion. Serve at once.

CREAMY TOMATO SOUP

Serves 6 children or 4 adults

I've made this easy and delicious soup for my family and whipped it up for as many as 200 children in no time at all. It was always a big hit at the healthy school lunch programme I started at my children's school. Double cream gives it silkiness and sheen, but you can make it dairy-free for the lactose-intolerant without any compromise in flavour by substituting coconut milk.

3 TABLESPOONS UNSALTED BUTTER OR EXTRA-VIRGIN OLIVE OIL, OR A COMBINATION

1 ONION, CHOPPED

500G TINNED PEELED PLUM TOMATOES IN NATURAL JUICES

10 FRESH BASIL LEAVES

2 SPRIGS FRESH FLAT-LEAF PARSLEY

120G DOUBLE CREAM, OR SUBSTITUTE COCONUT MILK

½ TEASPOON SEA SALT, OR TO TASTE

FRESHLY GROUND WHITE PEPPER

1. In a large saucepan, warm the butter or olive oil, or a mixture, if using. Add the onion and sauté over medium heat until the onion is completely soft, about 7 minutes. Stir in the tomatoes and their juices, the basil and the parsley. Simmer over medium-low heat until the mixture becomes concentrated and aromatic, about 15 minutes. Turn off the heat.

2. Use a hand blender to puree the tomato mixture until silky. Alternatively, leave the mixture to cool somewhat and purée it in a blender in batches, or pass it through a food mill. Return the liquid to the pan and bring to a simmer. Stir in the cream or coconut milk and heat through. Whether using cream or coconut milk, don't allow the soup to boil once it is added; just season with salt and pepper, heat through and serve.

QUICK GRILLED CHEESE PANINI

Serves 4 children

The differences between American grilled cheese sandwiches and Italian panini lies in the types of fillings and cheeses used. Mozzarella and fontina are typical ingredients because they are, hands down, the best melting cheeses. Children love these panini in particular because they taste like pizza. For the most nutritious version, use wholemeal bread.

8 SLICES WHOLEGRAIN OR WHITE
SANDWICH LOAF BREAD, CRUSTS
REMOVED

EXTRA-VIRGIN OLIVE OIL, FOR BRUSHING

225G FRESH MOZZARELLA CUT INTO
8 THIN SLICES ABOUT 2.5CM SMALLER
THAN THE BREAD

1 FRESH, VINE-RIPENED TOMATO, CORED
AND CUT INTO THIN STRIPS

DRIED OREGANO

SEA SALT

1. Place the slices of bread on a chopping board. Use a pastry brush to spread olive oil lightly over both sides of each slice. Select a frying pan large enough to accommodate 8 slices of bread. Alternatively, use a frying pan that can accommodate 4 bread slices and make the sandwiches in two batches. Warm the frying pan over medium heat for 4 minutes. Place the bread slices in the pan and cook until crisp and light golden brown on one side only, about 3 minutes. Transfer the bread slices to your work surface, crisp side up.

2. Place half of the cheese slices in the centre of half the bread slices. Distribute the tomatoes on top, then sprinkle with oregano and salt to taste. Lay the remaining cheese slices over that. Top with the remaining slices of bread, crisp side down, pressing down gently to set.

3. Warm the frying pan once again over low heat. Transfer each sandwich into the pan and place a weight, such as a smaller pan or a plate topped with a heavy tin, on top. Cook until crisp and deep golden brown, 2 to 3 minutes per side, then flip the sandwiches back to the first side to reheat and crisp, about 15 seconds. Serve.

FRESH
ROOT VEGETABLE PURÉE

Makes 68oz

Root vegetables are packed with nutrients and minerals, and babies love their natural sweetness. Use this method to make a creamy baby food of carrots, parsnips or other vegetables – or a delicious vegetable course for the whole family.

700G FRESH CARROTS OR PARSNIPS   1 LITRE WATER, PLUS MORE IF NEEDED

4 TABLESPOONS UNSALTED BUTTER

1. Scrape the carrots or parsnips and slice thin.

2. In a saucepan, melt the butter over medium heat. Stir in the carrots or parsnips and the water. Cover and cook until the liquid reduces to about 3 tablespoons and the vegetable is thoroughly softened, about 45 minutes, stirring occasionally. Add a little more water, if necessary, to prevent the purée from drying out.

3. Transfer the carrots or parsnips to a blender or food-processor and purée until creamy. Spoon the purée into a food mill or a sieve, pressing to pass the vegetable through the holes. Season as you like with a little more butter or extra-virgin olive oil before serving.

FUSILLI
WITH CREAMY CHEESE SAUCE

Serves 4 children or 2 adults

My children were mad about this simple pasta dish when they were growing up. They begged for it at every meal, and they always wanted to introduce it to every new friend who came for lunch or dinner. It even became standard birthday party fare, by request. The recipe has travelled to more children's households than I can remember, so I offer it here. I use mascarpone, an Italian cream cheese, but it can be made successfully with any other good-quality cream cheese.

225G IMPORTED ITALIAN FUSILLI ('CORKSCREW'), RADIATORE ('LITTLE RADIATOR'), OR CONCHIGLIE ('SHELLS'), OR OTHER SHORT-CUT PASTA

1 TABLESPOON KOSHER SALT

3 TABLESPOONS UNSALTED BUTTER, SOFTENED

110G MASCARPONE OR GOOD-QUALITY CREAM CHEESE, AT ROOM TEMPERATURE

2 TABLESPOONS FRESHLY GRATED PARMIGIANO-REGGIANO OR GRANA PADANO CHEESE

1. Bring 4.7 litres water to the boil and stir in the pasta and salt at once. Cook it according to the packet directions.

2. Meanwhile, in a double boiler or saucepan over very low heat, melt the butter and stir in the mascarpone or cream cheese, using a whisk to blend. Remove from the heat.

3. Drain the pasta, reserving 60ml of the cooking water, and while it is still dripping wet, combine the pasta with the sauce in a serving bowl, tossing to coat the pasta. If necessary, add the reserved cooking water to moisten. Add the grated cheese and toss again. Serve immediately.

PASTINA 'STARS'
WITH BUTTER AND MILK

Serves 4 children or 2 adults

Nothing is more emblematic of an Italian childhood than *pastina* (literally, 'little pasta') with butter and milk. It is baby's first solid food, remembered in adulthood with great nostalgia. There are many different varieties of *pastina*, including *anellini* ('little rings'), *stelline* ('little stars'), *acini de pepe* ('peppercorns'), *funghetti* ('little mushrooms'), *alfabeti* ('alphabets'), and *orzo* ('barley'), to name a few of the most common. For best results, save some of the cooking water after draining and add it as needed after stirring in the butter and milk to keep the pastina moist and fluid.

150G 'LITTLE STARS' PASTINA OR OTHER TINY PASTINA SHAPES

3 TEASPOONS SALT

3 TABLESPOONS UNSALTED BUTTER

125ML WARM MILK, PLUS MORE IF DESIRED

1. Bring 2.8 litres water to the boil. Stir in the pastina and salt. Cook according to the packet directions. Drain and transfer to a bowl.

2. While still piping hot, add butter to the pasta, burying it in the pasta to melt. Stir in warm milk and serve at once. Add a little more warm milk for a looser texture if desired. Serve immediately to prevent the pastina from drying out and clumping.

QUICK LINGUINE AND TOMATO LUNCH
Serves 4 children or 2 adults

Here is a surprising recipe from the Coluccio family, founders of the noteworthy Italian grocery in Brooklyn named Coluccio & Sons – surprising because from a few ordinary ingredients, most of them from the pantry, comes an astonishingly good dish. It is one of those quick dishes that is prepared for hungry children almost instantly and becomes a fond memory of childhood – and a standby in adult life. It works best in small quantities for 450g or less of pasta. Because some of the pasta water serves as a vehicle for the sauce, the dish needs to be eaten immediately while it is still very moist.

8 WHOLE FRESH OR TINNED PEELED PLUM TOMATOES, DRAINED

225G IMPORTED ITALIAN LINGUINE OR SPAGHETTI, BROKEN IN HALF

3 TABLESPOONS KOSHER SALT

6 FRESH BASIL LEAVES, IF AVAILABLE, CHOPPED

4 TABLESPOONS EXTRA-VIRGIN OLIVE OIL

4 TABLESPOONS FRESHLY GRATED PECORINO ROMANO, CACIOCAVALLO, PARMIGIANO-REGGIANO OR GRANA PADANO CHEESE

1. Bring 2.4 litres water to a rolling boil. Slip in the whole tomatoes and cook for 1 minute. Add the pasta and salt to the water and cook until it is al dente, or according to the directions on the pasta box. Drain the pasta and the tomatoes and reserve about 60ml of the pasta cooking water. While the pasta is still dripping wet, transfer it along with the tomatoes to an individual serving dishes.

2. Use a fork to mash up the tomatoes, mixing them with the basil leaves. Add about 1 tablespoon of the reserved pasta water to each serving to moisten the pasta if necessary. Top with the olive oil and cheese and serve at once.

SWEET or SAVOURY RICE
COOKED IN MILK

Serves 4 children or 2 adults

Venetian-born Nicoletta Polo is a direct descendant of Marco Polo and takes great pride in her Venetian legacy. She suggested this creamy dish, which Venetian children eat with sugar for breakfast, for an after-school snack or even for dinner. It is digestible, nourishing and delicious. You'll need to buy Venetian or other short-grained Italian rice, of which there are three types available: *Vialone Nano* (Veneto rice), *Arborio* or *Carnaroli*. The family of medium-to-short-grain rices, to which these varieties belong, has the attribute of being able to absorb large quantities of liquid, little by little, without turning to mush. Be sure to add the salt only after cooking to avoid inadvertently oversalting. Savoury and sweet versions are included.

950ML MILK

220G VIALONE NANO, ARBORIO OR
CARNAROLI SHORT-GRAIN RICE

½ TEASPOON SEA SALT, OR TO TASTE

FOR THE SAVOURY VERSION

UNSALTED BUTTER

FRESHLY GRATED PARMIGIANO-REGGIANO
CHEESE (OPTIONAL)

FOR THE SWEET VERSION

SUGAR

1. If you are making the savoury version, the quantities called for should stand. If you are making the sweet version, however, it should not be as soupy but, instead, *all'onda,* 'wavelike', more like a risotto. To achieve this, decrease the milk by about 125ml, or increase the rice by 55g. If you are making the plain version, neither savoury nor sweet, the quantities should also stand.

2. In a saucepan, bring the milk to a gentle boil over medium-low heat. Stir in the rice and salt. Simmer, stirring occasionally, until the rice is soft, about 10 minutes. Season to taste with the butter and cheese, if using, for the savoury version or with the sugar for the sweet version, or eat without seasoning.

TOMATO RICE
WITH MOZZARELLA DICE

Serves 4 to 6 children

This way of cooking rice is called *riso all'Inglese,* 'English-style rice', because it is boiled plain, not cooked with a sauce, like a risotto. It was a standby when I was growing up, though it was elaborated on slightly from the original white version with a touch of tomato sauce for colour and small pieces of mozzarella. Once folded into the hot rice, the cheese formed long, oozy strands that were fun to eat. If using short-grain rice, follow the method for cooking here; if using a long-grain variety, cook according to the packet instructions instead and fold the sauce and cheese in at the end.

220G SHORT-GRAIN RICE SUCH AS ARBORIO, CARNAROLI OR VIALONE NANO, OR LONG-GRAIN RICE

SEA SALT

55G DICED SMOKED MOZZARELLA OR FRESH MOZZARELLA

2 TABLESPOONS PREPARED TOMATO SAUCE SUCH AS FRUITY NEAPOLITAN TOMATO SAUCE (PAGE 34) OR 20-MINUTE TOMATO SAUCE (PAGE 37), PURÉED

1 TABLESPOON UNSALTED BUTTER (OPTIONAL)

1. In a saucepan, bring 750ml water to a rapid boil. Stir in the rice and a pinch of salt and cover. Cook until done, about 20 minutes.

2. When the rice is cooked, turn off the heat and fold in the cheese, the tomato sauce and the butter, if using. Serve at once.

12
BASICS

It is a widely accepted notion in Italy that the best cooking is found at home. This is due more to quality and craftsmanship than artistry. The Italian approach is simple. There are a few rudimentary techniques for the application of heat – sautéing, searing, frying, braising, stewing and roasting, which are described in recipe methods and are easy to follow. A few stocks, sauces, basic doughs and condiments included in this chapter are indispensable. None is elaborate or requires lengthy preparation. The basics described are best homemade because store-bought versions bear little similarity in flavour or goodness. Pre-cooked polenta, solidified and packed in a cellophane tube can be purchased, but it can't compare with what steaming fresh polenta looks like, tastes like and smells like, or with the way it behaves under a sauce and on the tongue. In short, nothing can replace what good quality does for cooking. Or as the Italians say, 'Good with good makes good'.

TASTY MEAT STOCK

Makes 2.5 litres

Meat stock can provide a delicious starting point for soups. It can also add flavour and moisture to sauces and stews. For maximum flavour, the meat and vegetables should start out cooking in cold water. This way, the meat juices are released into the stock rather than being sealed in by immediate application of intense heat. The best stock is made with a combination of meats.

900G CHICKEN BACKS OR WINGS

900G BEEF BRAISING STEAK OR FORESHANK OR SHORT RIBS

2 LARGE LEEKS

900G VEAL NECK BONES

2 MEDIUM FRESH OR TINNED TOMATOES

2 ONIONS, UNPEELED AND WASHED, QUARTERED

3 LARGE CARROTS, SCRAPED AND CUT INTO QUARTERS

3 LARGE CELERY STICKS, INCLUDING LEAVES

1 BUNCH FLAT-LEAF PARSLEY, STEMS AND LEAVES

1 TEASPOON WHOLE PEPPERCORNS

KOSHER SALT OR SEA SALT

1. Wash the chicken well, removing any excess fat, but keep the skin on. Remove any excess fat from the beef. Trim the root from the leek, slice the leek lengthwise, and spread open the sheaths under the running water to remove any sand. Slice into 1-inch pieces.

2. Select a large saucepan into which all the meat will fit comfortably. Add all of the other ingredients except for the salt. Add 2.5 litres cold water. Cover the pan and bring to the boil. Immediately reduce to medium-low and adjust the heat if necessary to keep the stock at a gentle simmer. Leave the pan partially covered. Skim any foam that forms on the surface. Simmer until full-bodied and tasty, about 4 hours from the boil. The stock should not return to the boil.

3. When the stock is finished, skim off any fat that has risen to the surface. Remove the meat and bones (use the meat for some other purpose). Pass the stock through a fine-mesh sieve. Add salt to taste just before using.

AHEAD-OF-TIME NOTE: This stock can be made up to 4 days in advance. Strain out the meat and vegetables, cover and refrigerate for up to 4 days, or freeze for up to 3 months. When you are ready to use it, add the salt.

CHICKEN STOCK

Makes 2.5 litres

Use free-range or organic chickens; they have been raised without the antibiotics and other non-food additives of the cage-bred variety and produce a better-tasting stock than do industrially raised chickens. For a rich taste, the proportion of meat to water should be generous.

2.25KG CHICKEN WINGS OR BACKS

2 BAY LEAVES

2 MEDIUM ONIONS, UNPEELED AND QUARTERED

2 LARGE CARROTS, SCRAPED AND CUT INTO EIGHT PIECES

2 LARGE CELERY STICKS, INCLUDING LEAVES

2 MEDIUM FRESH OR TINNED TOMATOES

1 SMALL BUNCH FLAT-LEAF PARSLEY, STEMS AND LEAVES

110G PEELED CELERIAC, IF AVAILABLE

2 TEASPOONS WHOLE BLACK OR WHITE PEPPERCORNS

SEA SALT

1. Wash the chicken well, removing any excess fat.

2. Select a large saucepan into which the chicken parts will fit comfortably, but not much wider. Put in all of the ingredients except the salt. Add 2.5 litres cold water. Cover and bring to the boil. Immediately reduce to medium-low and check occasionally, adjusting the heat if necessary to keep the stock at a gentle simmer. Leave the pan partially covered. Skim the surface whenever scum forms. Simmer until the meat falls off the bones, about 90 minutes from the boil.

3. Strain the stock through a fine-mesh sieve. Pick the meat off the bones and reserve for some other purpose. Discard the other solids. Leave the stock to cool at room temperature, then cover and refrigerate for up to 3 days, or freeze for up to 3 months. Add salt to taste just before using.

VEGETABLE STOCK

Makes about 2 litres

Despite their being vegetarians, my children crave the intense flavours of genuine Italian cooking, so I always have rich-tasting vegetable stock on hand as a foundation for soups and other dishes where stock is called for. I have found that sautéeing the vegetables in butter or olive oil prior to cooking produces a tastier stock rather than strictly boiling them.

1 LARGE LEEK, OR 3 BUNCHES SPRING ONIONS

3 TABLESPOONS UNSALTED BUTTER OR EXTRA-VIRGIN OLIVE OIL

3 CARROTS, SCRAPED AND SLICED

2 ONIONS, DICED

2 LARGE CELERY STICKS, PLUS THE LEAVES FROM THE WHOLE CELERY HEAD

2 LARGE BAY LEAVES

2 LITRES WATER

1 TEASPOON BLACK PEPPERCORNS

1 TEASPOON ALLSPICE BERRIES

A HANDFUL OF FLAT-LEAF PARSLEY, LEAVES AND STEMS

1 TABLESPOON SEA SALT, OR TO TASTE

1. Trim off and discard the roots and discoloured parts of the stem of the leek. Slice the leek in half lengthways and spread open the sheaths under cold running water to wash out any sand that is lodged between them. Slice into 1-inch pieces crossways.

2. In a large saucepan over medium-low heat, melt the butter or warm the olive oil. Add the leek, carrots, onion, celery sticks and their leaves, and bay leaves. Sauté the vegetables gently without letting them brown, about 10 minutes. Add 250ml of the water, stir and cover. Cook gently for an additional 20 minutes, stirring occasionally.

3. Add the remaining 1.75 litres water, the peppercorns, allspice and parsley. Cover and cook over low heat for 1½ hours. Strain through a fine-mesh strainer. Season with the salt.

AHEAD-OF-TIME NOTE: This stock can be made 2 or 3 days in advance of using, cooled, covered and refrigerated. Or it can be frozen for up to 3 months.

RAPHAEL BOERI'S
MILK DOUGH FOR YEAST BREAD
For 1 focaccia, 2 pizzas, or 2 breads

Raphael Boeri is a French pastry chef who spent many years working in Italy learning the breadmaker's art. His yeast dough, learned from a Milanese baker and *pizzaiolo*, incorporates milk and egg, resulting in a tender, richly flavoured crust with a crispy skin. When I first ate it in a rustic *pissaladella* (page 22) that Raphael created for the Didier Dumas Patisserie in my village, it was a revelation to me. You can use it for any pizza, focaccia or yeast bread base, whether baked or fried – or for loaf bread. Note that a tablespoon and a half of beaten egg is called for, as measurements need to be precise. You can easily double the recipe, using a total of one large egg to make measuring easier. Then divide the dough in half and freeze the portion you don't use immediately.

200ML OR MORE WARM WATER	25ML MILK, AT ROOM TEMPERATURE
2 TABLESPOONS EASY BLEND YEAST OR 15G FRESH BAKER'S YEAST	500G UNBLEACHED PLAIN FLOUR
75ML EXTRA-VIRGIN OLIVE OIL	2 TEASPOONS SEA SALT
1½ TABLESPOONS BEATEN EGG	PINCH OF SUGAR

1. Place 130g warm water in a medium bowl. Stir in the yeast. Leave the mixture to stand in a warm place until it becomes foamy, about 10 minutes.

2. In another bowl, combine the remaining warm water, the olive oil, beaten egg and milk.

3. In the bowl of an electric mixer fitted with a dough hook, combine the flour, salt, and sugar. Turn the mixer on low and mix until the dough is smooth and somewhat sticky, 6 to 7 minutes, stopping occasionally to scrape down the sides and base of the bowl. Add 1 to 2 teaspoons more warm water as necessary to make a dough that is cohesive and smooth, but still lightly sticky to the touch.

4. Place the dough in a lightly oiled bowl. Lightly brush the dough with some oil. Cover completely with dampened clean tea towels. Allow to rise at room temperature in a draft-free location until doubled in size, about 45 minutes. The dough can now be formed into *pissaladella* (page 22), pizza, calzone (page 20), or loaves. For *pissaladella* or calzone, the dough does not need to rise again. For bread, form the dough into braided or rounded loaves, cover with dampened tea towels and leave to rise until doubled in size. Preheat the oven to 200°C/400°F/gas mark 6 and bake until done, about 20 minutes.

BASIC POLENTA

Serves 6

Probably few things are more reminiscent of Italian home cooking than polenta, which is nothing more than a cornmeal porridge. In its simplest guise, it is served in that form with butter and a hard grating cheese, or with a soft, runny cheese (see Steaming Polenta with Taleggio Cheese, page 106). Or it can be topped with a meat or mushroom sauce or a stew; a particularly happy union is polenta with Viola Buitoni's Long-Simmered Tomato Sauce with Ribs and Sausages (page 42). Polenta can also be turned out onto a marble slab or another hard surface, allowed to become firm, then cut into squares. These pieces have endless uses, especially for antipasti. Whether fried or sautéed in olive oil, or brushed with olive oil and grilled, they become *crostini di polenta,* delicious crunchy 'toasts'. Note that polenta must be made from polenta cornmeal.

1.75 LITRES WATER	300G POLENTA CORNMEAL
1 TABLESPOON KOSHER SALT	BOILING WATER, AS NEEDED

1. Bring the water to the boil in a deep saucepan. Add the salt and bring the heat down to medium. Then add the cornmeal very slowly, almost in a trickle (*a doccia,* 'like a shower'); this gradual introduction of cornmeal to the boiling water prevents lumps from forming. Keep the polenta at a constant simmer and, from the instant the cornmeal is added to the water, continuously stir it with a long-handled wooden spoon or whisk, always in the same direction. After all the cornmeal is absorbed, continue to stir until the polenta is thick and pulls away easily from the sides of the pan. If the polenta is quite thick but still not pulling, add a little more boiling water and continue to stir until it is ready. It should be perfectly cooked, thick and creamy in 25 to 30 minutes.

2. If serving loose, pour into a platter at once, dress according to your recipe and serve. For polenta crostini, pour the hot polenta out onto a clean oiled work surface and use a rubber fish slice to spread to a thickness of 5mm. Leave it to set and grill or fry, as preferred.

HOMEMADE MAYONNAISE
WITH VARIATIONS

Makes 220g

There is no equal to homemade mayonnaise, and it is very easy to prepare with a blender. It is important that your utensils be warm and that all the ingredients be at room temperature, that is, out of the fridge for an hour or more. While classic recipes for mayonnaise call for two egg yolks, for this quantity of oil, I like to use a whole egg instead. It makes the mayonnaise lighter and more nutritious (egg white is pure protein). Use this light, silky dressing (see variations below) on freshly boiled meat or vegetables, steamed lobster or warm boiled potatoes, just to name a few possibilities.

125ML GRAPESEED OIL OR OTHER VEGETABLE OIL

60ML EXTRA-VIRGIN OLIVE OIL

1 LARGE EGG, AT ROOM TEMPERATURE

½ TEASPOON SALT, OR TO TASTE

2 TABLESPOONS FRESHLY SQUEEZED LEMON JUICE, OR TO TASTE

1 TEASPOON DIJON MUSTARD

DASH OF FRESHLY GROUND WHITE PEPPER

Combine the oils in a small jug. Crack the egg into the blender and pulse for 3 seconds. Add 2 tablespoons of the oils. Blend on high speed for 10 seconds. With the machine running, add the remaining oil in a very thin, slow, steady stream. Turn off the blender and use a rubber spatula to scrape the inside so that all the ingredients are thoroughly combined. Stir the salt into the lemon juice and add it with the mustard and pepper. Blend to combine thoroughly. Use immediately, or cover and chill. Homemade mayonnaise will keep for a week in the fridge.

NOTE: If the mayonnaise separates, bring it and an egg to room temperature. Break the yolk into a mixing bowl and whisk in the broken mayonnaise tablespoon by tablespoon until the mixture is cohesive, then add in a bit of whichever oil you used to set the mayonnaise to thin the consistency to your liking.

FOR GARLIC MAYONNAISE: Finely chop 3 large garlic cloves, then pound into a paste with a little salt and a pinch of cayenne pepper. Blend with 220g mayonnaise.

FOR LIGHT LEMON MAYONNAISE: Blend the mayonnaise with additional freshly squeezed lemon juice to taste. Thin with a little water until the mayonnaise reaches a pourable but still very creamy consistency.

FOR HORSERADISH MAYONNAISE: To 220g mayonnaise, blend a 5-cm piece of fresh horseradish root, grated, or 60g prepared white horseradish, or to taste, and 2 tablespoons Dijon mustard.

NEW WORLD
FLAKY PASTRY PIES
Makes 2 crusts or 16 tartlets

I call this 'New World' pastry dough because flaky pastries, which I love, are an English and American invention. When it comes to fruit pies, I much prefer them to the *pasta frolla*-type pastry of the Italians. This exceptional recipe was developed by my friend, food writer and pastry expert Susan G. Purdy. It is buttery in flavour, flaky in texture and incredibly easy to handle. This dough is most quickly prepared in a food-processor fitted with a steel blade. For best results, use a combination of frozen butter and well-chilled or frozen non-transfat vegetable fat (measure onto greaseproof paper and freeze about 30 minutes before starting). For a sweet pastry, add sugar and one large egg yolk as part of the measured liquid. For savoury meat fillings, omit the sugar and add one whole large egg.

375G PLAIN FLOUR

¾ TEASPOON SALT

OPTIONAL SWEETENER FOR SWEET PASTRY: 1½ TO 2 TABLESPOONS CASTER SUGAR

12 TABLESPOONS UNSALTED BUTTER, WELL CHILLED OR FROZEN, CUT UP

6 TABLESPOONS TRANS-FAT-FREE SOLID VEGETABLE FAT OR LARD, CHILLED OR FROZEN

1 LARGE EGG (OR ONE LARGE YOLK, SEE NOTE ABOVE)

1 TABLESPOON LEMON JUICE OR UNFLAVOURED VINEGAR

3 TO 5 TABLESPOONS ICE WATER, JUST AS NEEDED

EGG GLAZE (OPTIONAL)

1 WHOLE EGG BEATEN WITH 1 TEASPOON WATER

1. TO PREPARE PASTRY IN A FOOD-PROCESSOR: Combine flour, salt and sugar if used; pulse a few times to blend. Add the butter and solid vegetable fat and pulse only until fat is cut into bits the size of peas. Through the feed tube, add the egg and lemon juice or vinegar, pulse once or twice, then add ice water one tablespoon at a time, pulsing once or twice between additions, only until the pastry begins to show some clumps. Do not form a dough ball on the blade.

2. Turn the pastry out onto a piece of greaseproof paper (if it looks sandy and dry, sprinkle on a tiny bit more water) and use your hands to bring it together into a ball; the dough should hold the form of your fingers when squeezed. Wrap up the pastry and refrigerate for at least 30 minutes. To use, roll out on a lightly floured surface with a floured rolling pin. Note: if the butter and vegetable fat were frozen, the dough can be rolled without prior chilling.

OPTIONAL: To give a golden finish to the tops of pies or tartlets, use a pastry brush to coat them with the egg glaze just before baking.

INDEX

ACKNOWLEDGEMENTS

I am grateful to Anja Schmidt and to Kyle Cathie for the opportunity to write this book and to Carole Bidnick for shepherding it beyond what could be expected from any literary agent. And I thank my writing colleague, Bill Marsano, for his enthusiast support for this project at the outset and for his generous help with advice, information and writing.

It all began with a fine pile of handwritten recipes from my aunt and gifted cook, Rita Ghisu, who has comforted so many with her generous hospitality and remarkably good food; she is precisely the kind of cook to whom this book pays homage. So is Anna Amendolara Nurse, who besides offering her Pugliese recipes, which I love so much, has been a tireless mentor for over two decades, illuminating my professional path. For many comforting meals and for generously sharing her handwritten heirloom recipes, I am indebted to Anna Maria Weld.

Only my *amica stretta* and fellow author, Susan G. Purdy, knows the joys and torments of crafting a cookbook that you hope will convey what you want to say; I am so grateful for her advice.

I would also like to thank Nick Malgieri, Viola Buitoni, Donatella Platoni, Cathy Coluccio, Nicoletta Polo Lanza Tomasi, duchess of Palma, Baron Giuseppe Rosso, Rena Glickman, Nick Gualano, Didier Dumas and Raphael Boeri for research on my behalf and permission to reproduce their recipes; also to Sophie Giovanola, Lorraine Petrucci, Anna Palaia, Gina Quatrocchi, Francesco Fiondello and Olimpia Fiondello for sharing family recipes and for their efforts on my behalf; and to Mary Wallace, Joan Gussow, Barbara Bedway, and Greg Mitchell for tasting works in progress. Thanks are due also to Augusto Marchini and the Italian Trade Commission, Gruppo Ristoratori Italiani, and Oldways Preservation Trust for all I have learned during so many travels in Italy at their invitation. I am especially grateful to Flavia Destefanis for such generous research and Italian editing on yet another of my books; Laurel Robertson for months of recipe testing and help with field work; and Elizabeth Walber for working with me in the kindest and most generous way doing many hours of editing.

Perhaps the most thanks should go to the many Italian people whose names I never knew or cannot remember, who have offered their food and recipes with such generosity.

Having a visual bent, I believe that what makes a cookbook come alive besides its honesty are illustrations that can draw the reader in as few words alone can do. I am delighted with the exquisite photographs for this book that were taken by Christopher Hirsheimer and Melissa Hamilton, and that so perfectly express the simple goodness and timeless appeal of Italian comfort food.

Above all, I thank my good and beautiful children, Gabriella and Celina della Croce, for their constant support and enthusiasm for my cooking; Katie and Charlie Hoyt for their graceful presence at the new family table even if the food is sometimes exotic to them; and my husband Nathan Hoyt, who is an inexhaustible source of inspiration.